SHAKY KANE'S
MONSTER TRUCK

ROBERT KIRKMAN
COO

ERIK LARSEN
CFO

TODD McFARLANE
President

MARC SILVESTRI
CEO

JIM VALENTINO
Vice-President

ERIC STEPHENSON
Publisher

TODD MARTINEZ
Sales & Licensing Coordinator

SARAH DELAINE
PR & Marketing Coordinator

BRANWYN BIGGLESTONE
Accounts Manager

EMILY MILLER
Administrative Assistant

JAMIE PARRENO
Marketing Assistant

KEVIN YUEN
Digital Rights Coordinator

TYLER SHAINLINE
Production Manager

DREW GILL
Art Director

JONATHAN CHAN
Senior Production Artist

MONICA GARCIA
VINCENT KUKUA
JANA COOK
Production Artists

www.imagecomics.com

SHAKY KANE'S MONSTER TRUCK
ISBN: 978-1-60706-470-1
First Printing

I COULD RIDE THIS TRAIL BLINDFOLD

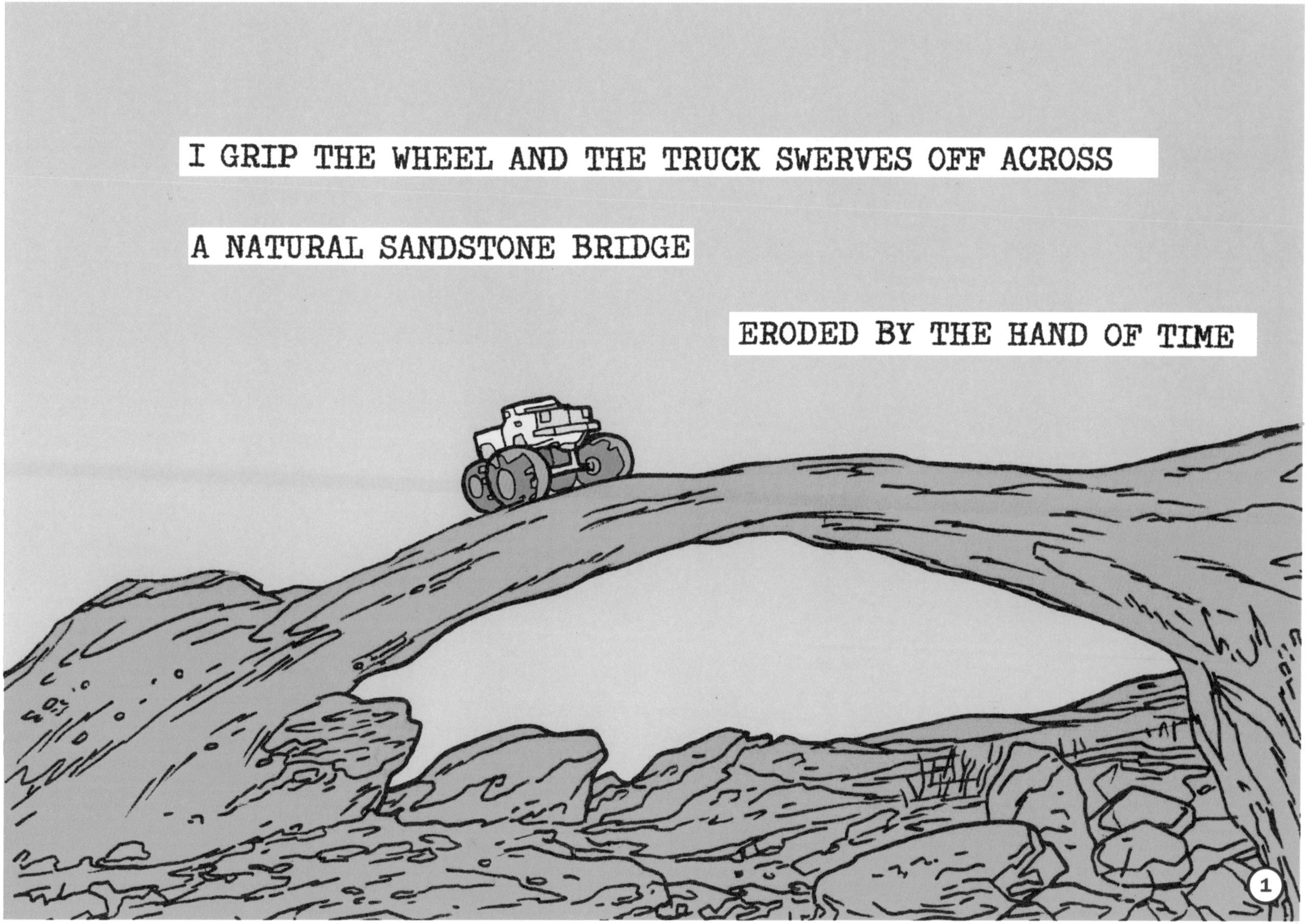
I GRIP THE WHEEL AND THE TRUCK SWERVES OFF ACROSS
A NATURAL SANDSTONE BRIDGE
ERODED BY THE HAND OF TIME

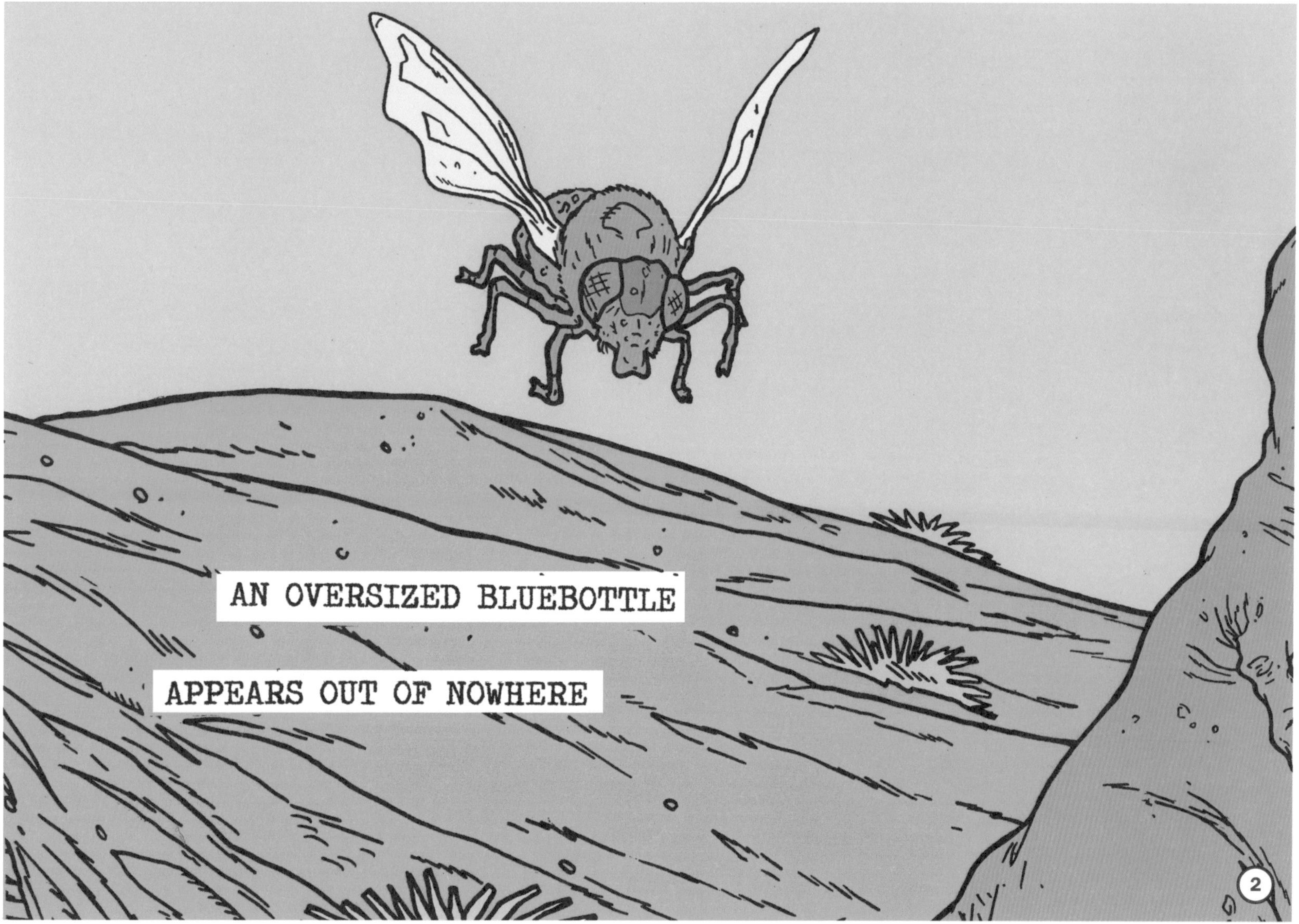
AN OVERSIZED BLUEBOTTLE
APPEARS OUT OF NOWHERE

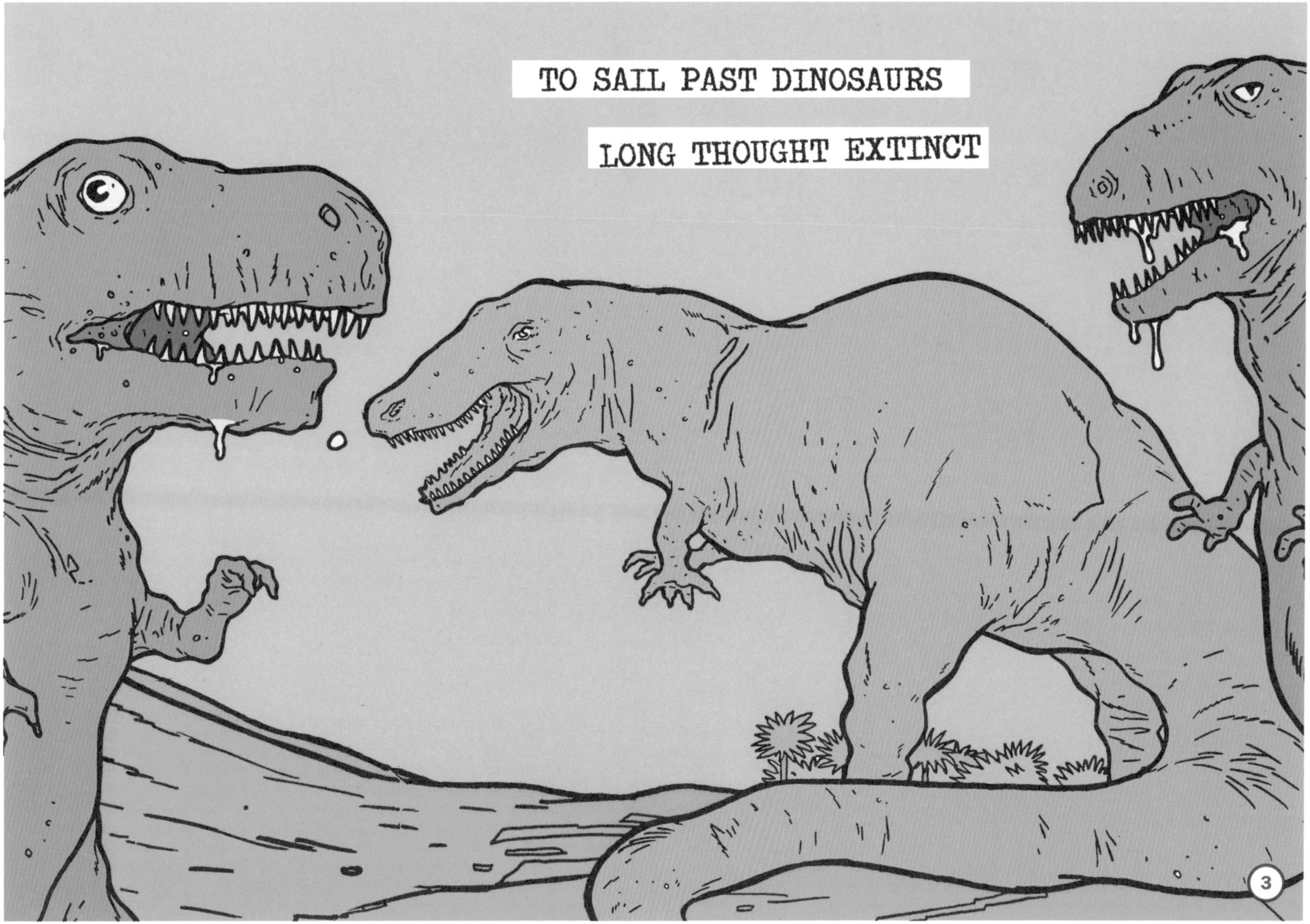
TO SAIL PAST DINOSAURS
LONG THOUGHT EXTINCT

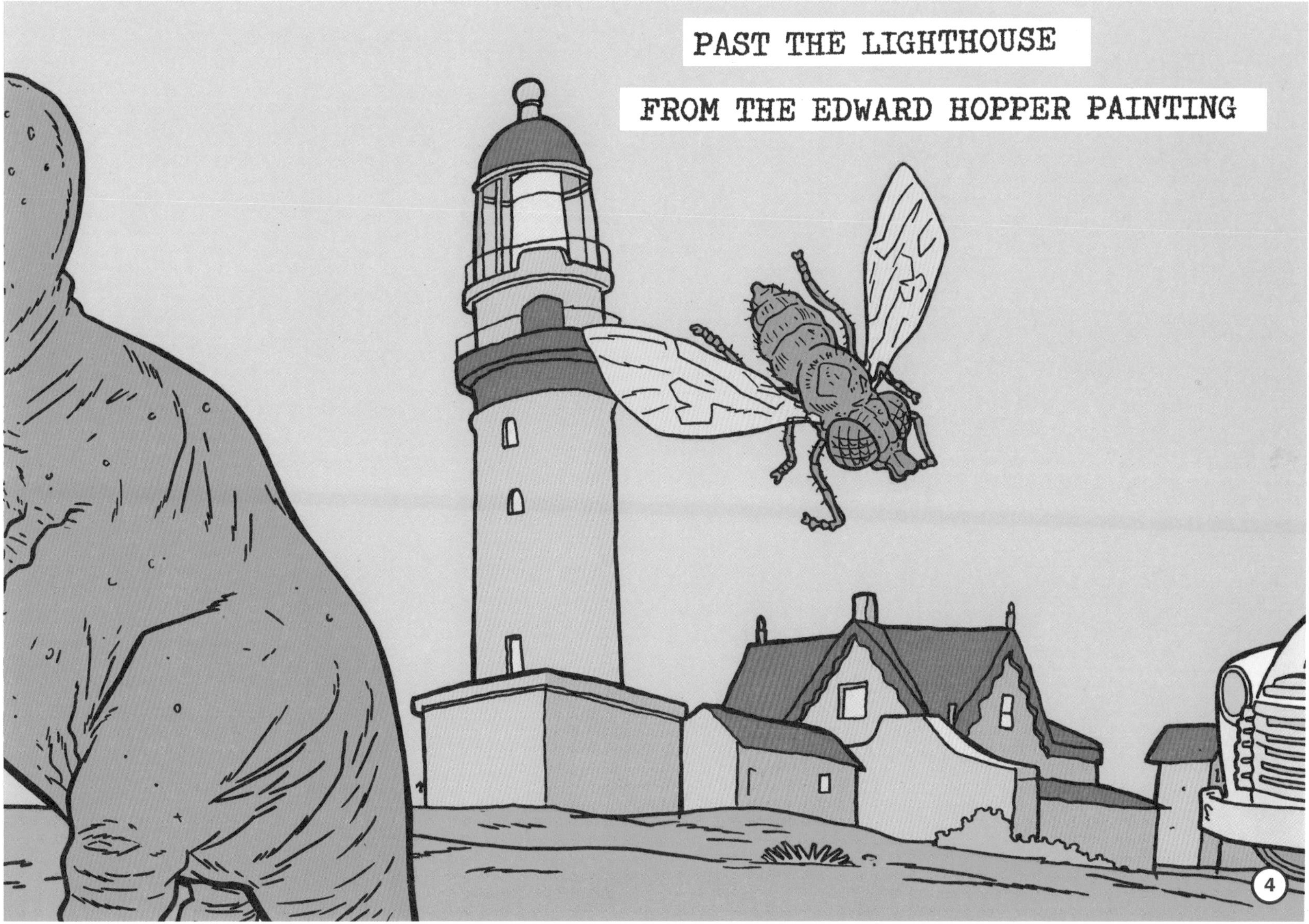
PAST THE LIGHTHOUSE
FROM THE EDWARD HOPPER PAINTING
4

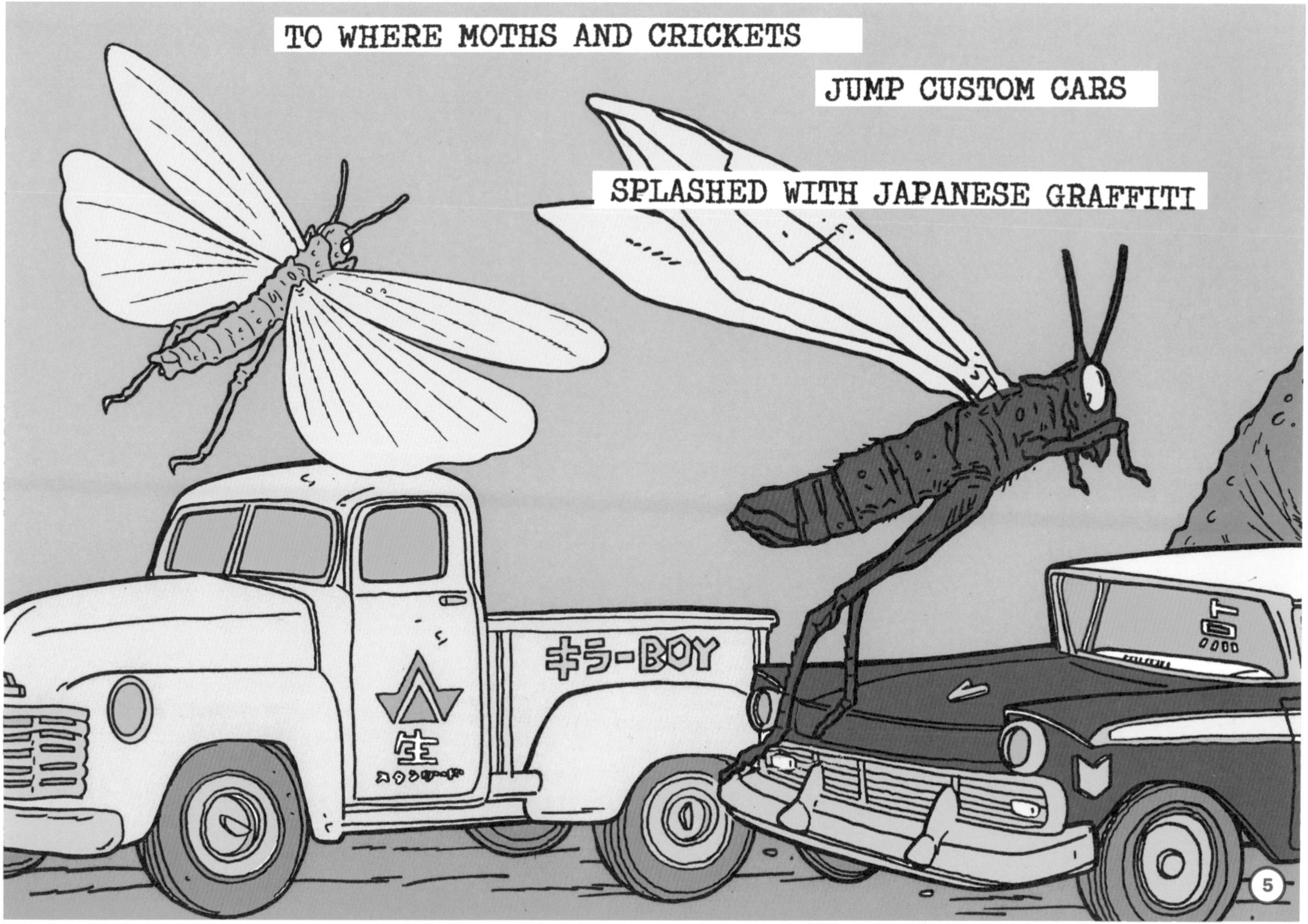
TO WHERE MOTHS AND CRICKETS
JUMP CUSTOM CARS
SPLASHED WITH JAPANESE GRAFFITI
キラーBOY
生

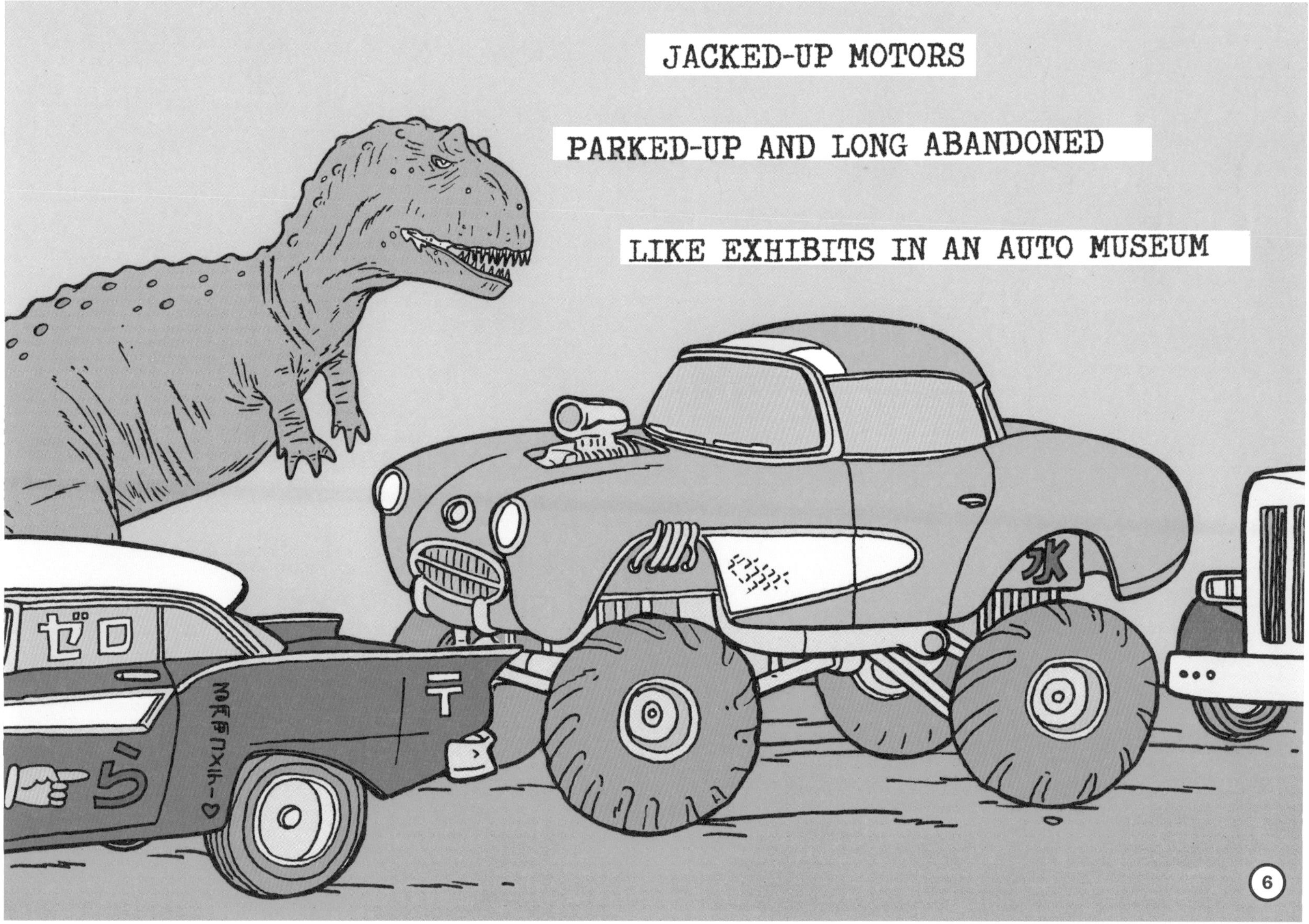
JACKED-UP MOTORS
PARKED-UP AND LONG ABANDONED
LIKE EXHIBITS IN AN AUTO MUSEUM
ゼロ
ら

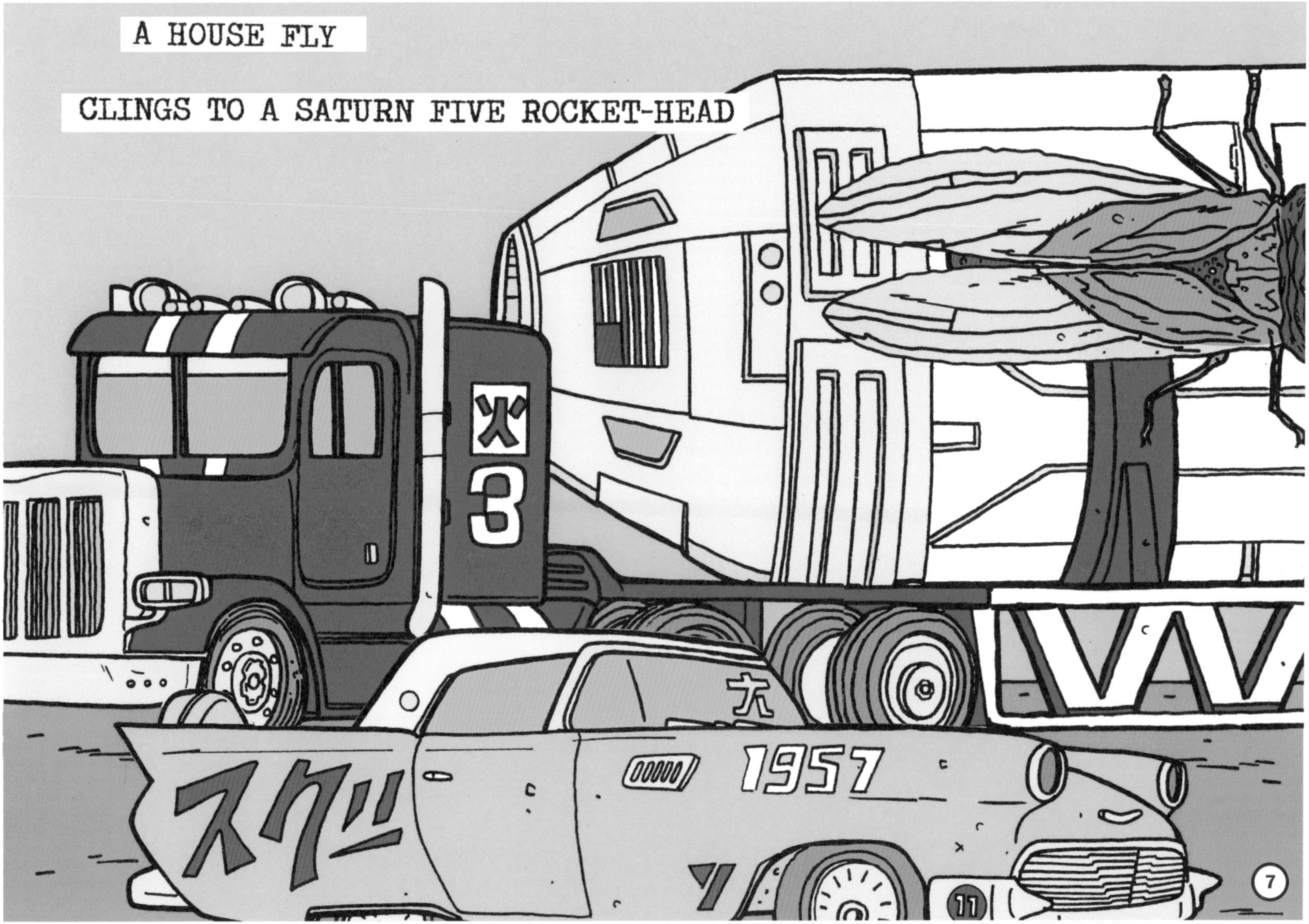
A HOUSE FLY
CLINGS TO A SATURN FIVE ROCKET-HEAD
3
1957

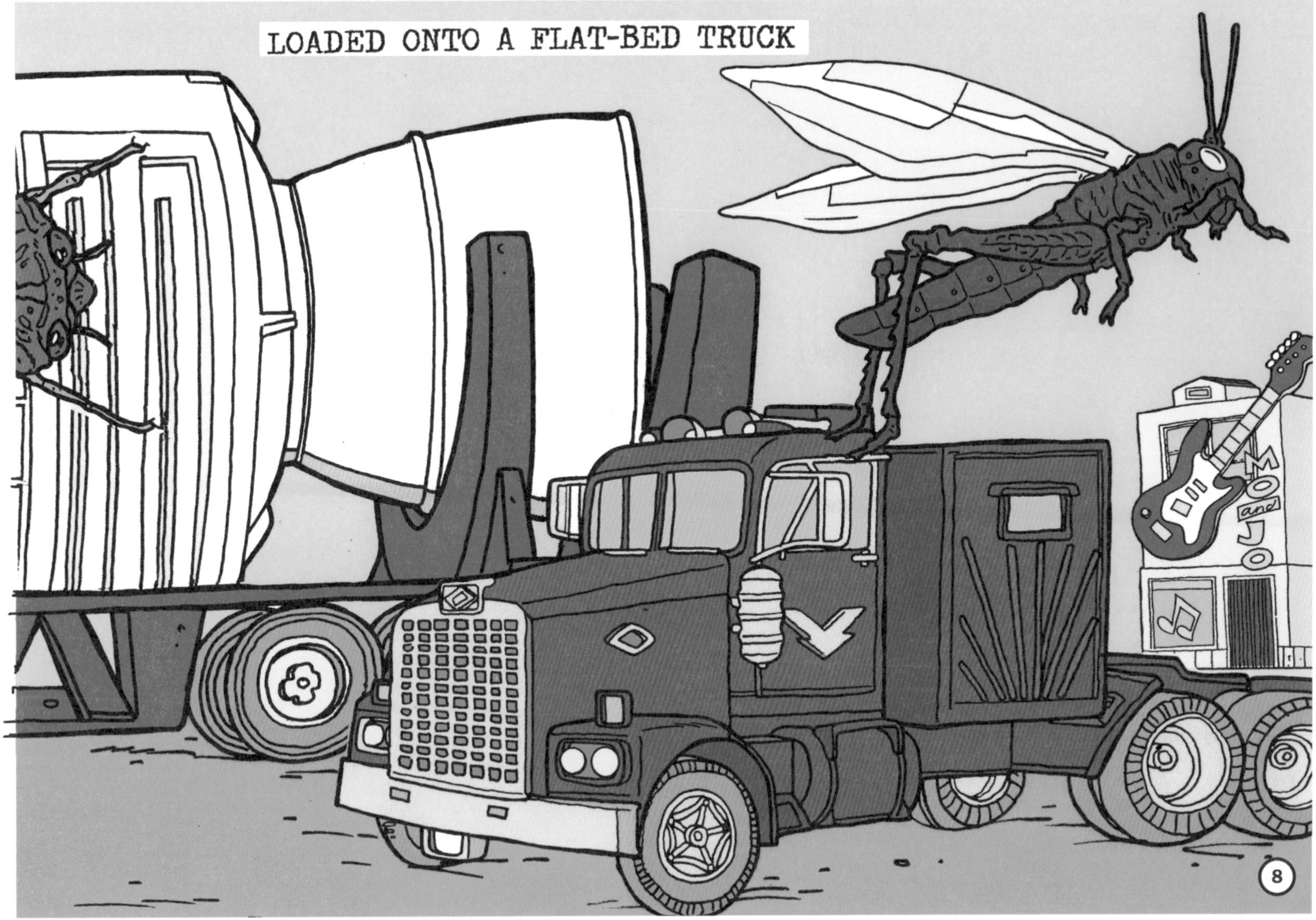
LOADED ONTO A FLAT-BED TRUCK
MOJO
and
JO

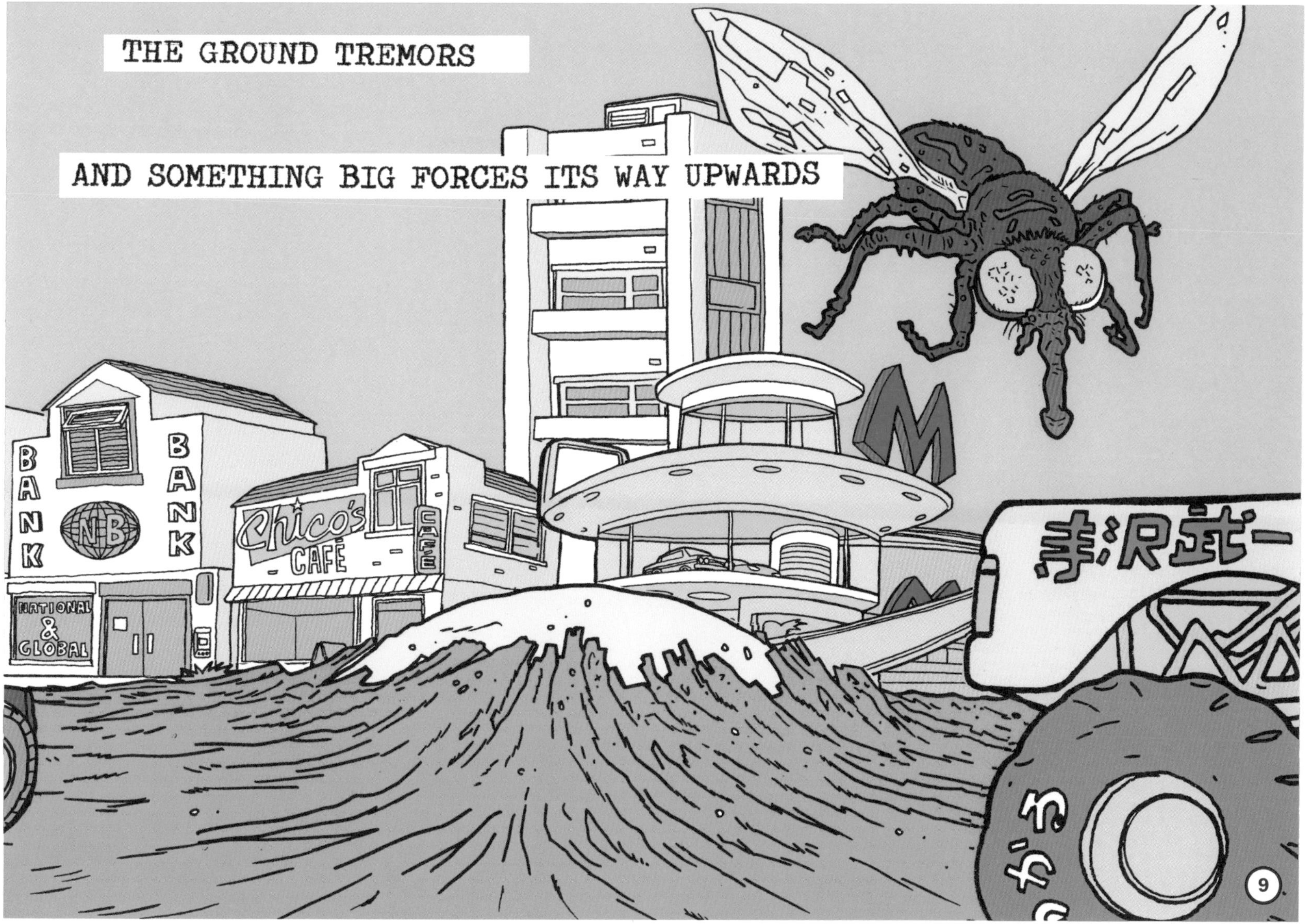

THE GROUND TREMORS
AND SOMETHING BIG FORCES ITS WAY UPWARDS
BANK
NB
BANK
NATIONAL & GLOBAL
Chico's CAFÉ
CAFE
M

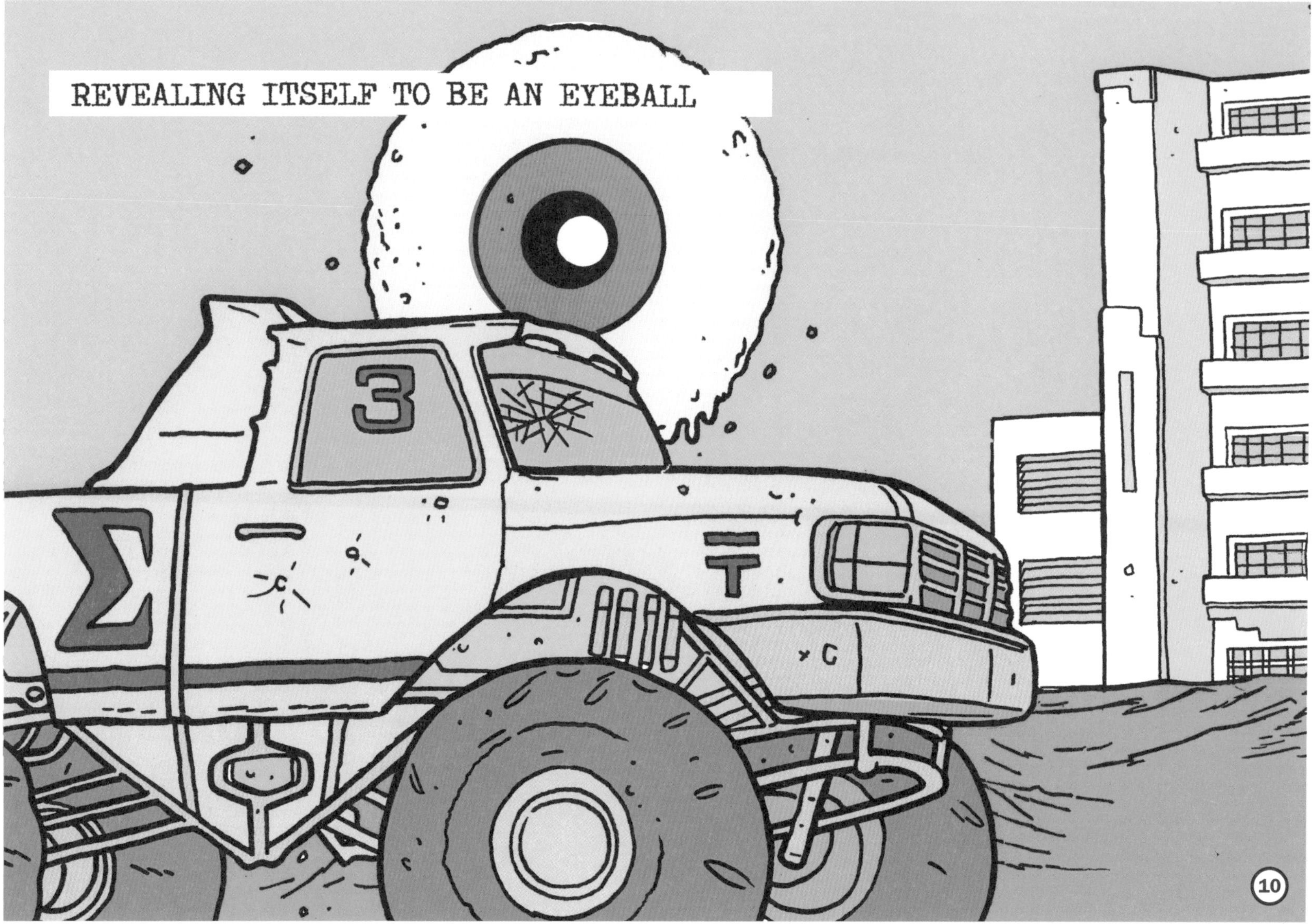
REVEALING ITSELF TO BE AN EYEBALL
3
Σ
10

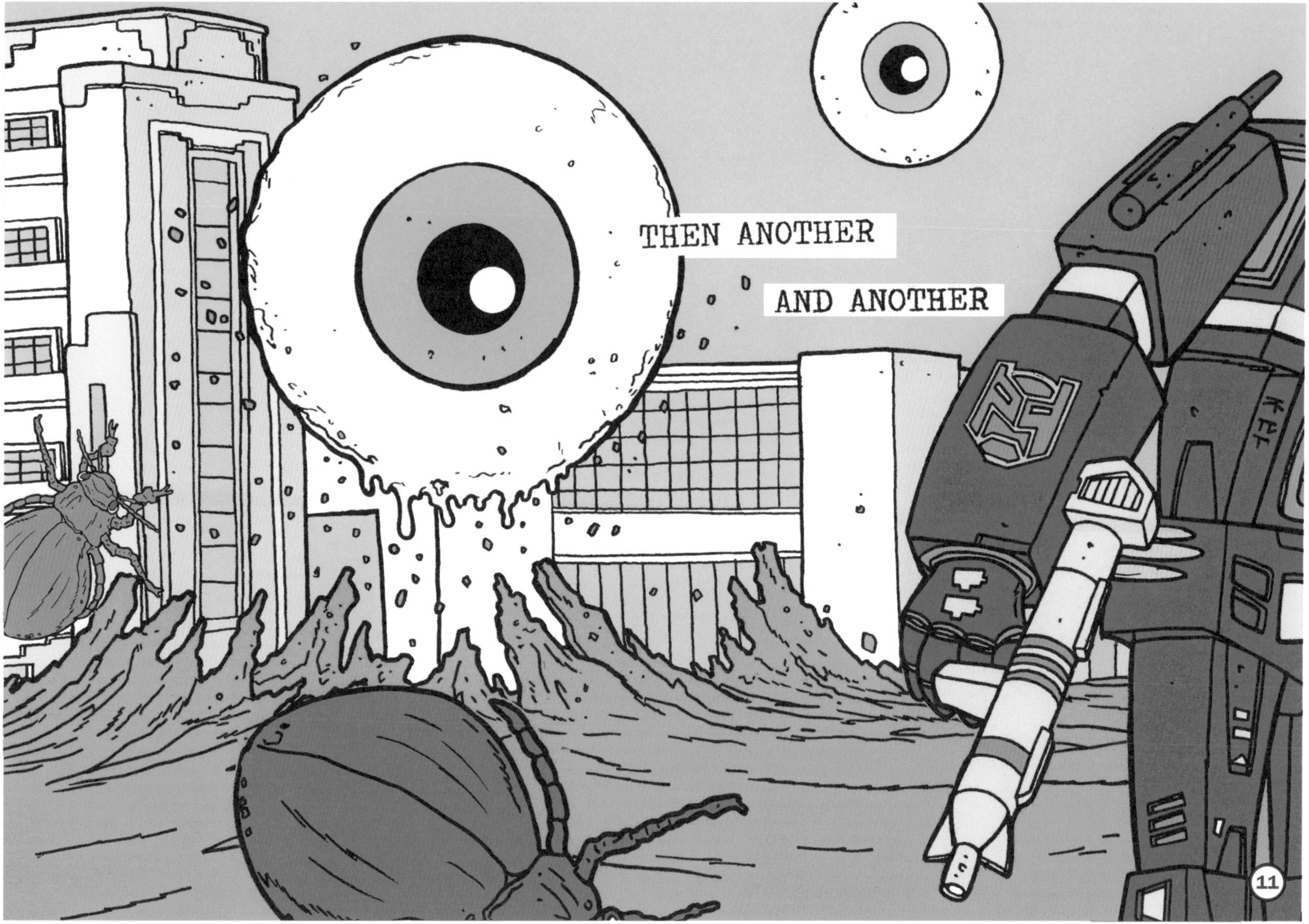
THEN ANOTHER
AND ANOTHER

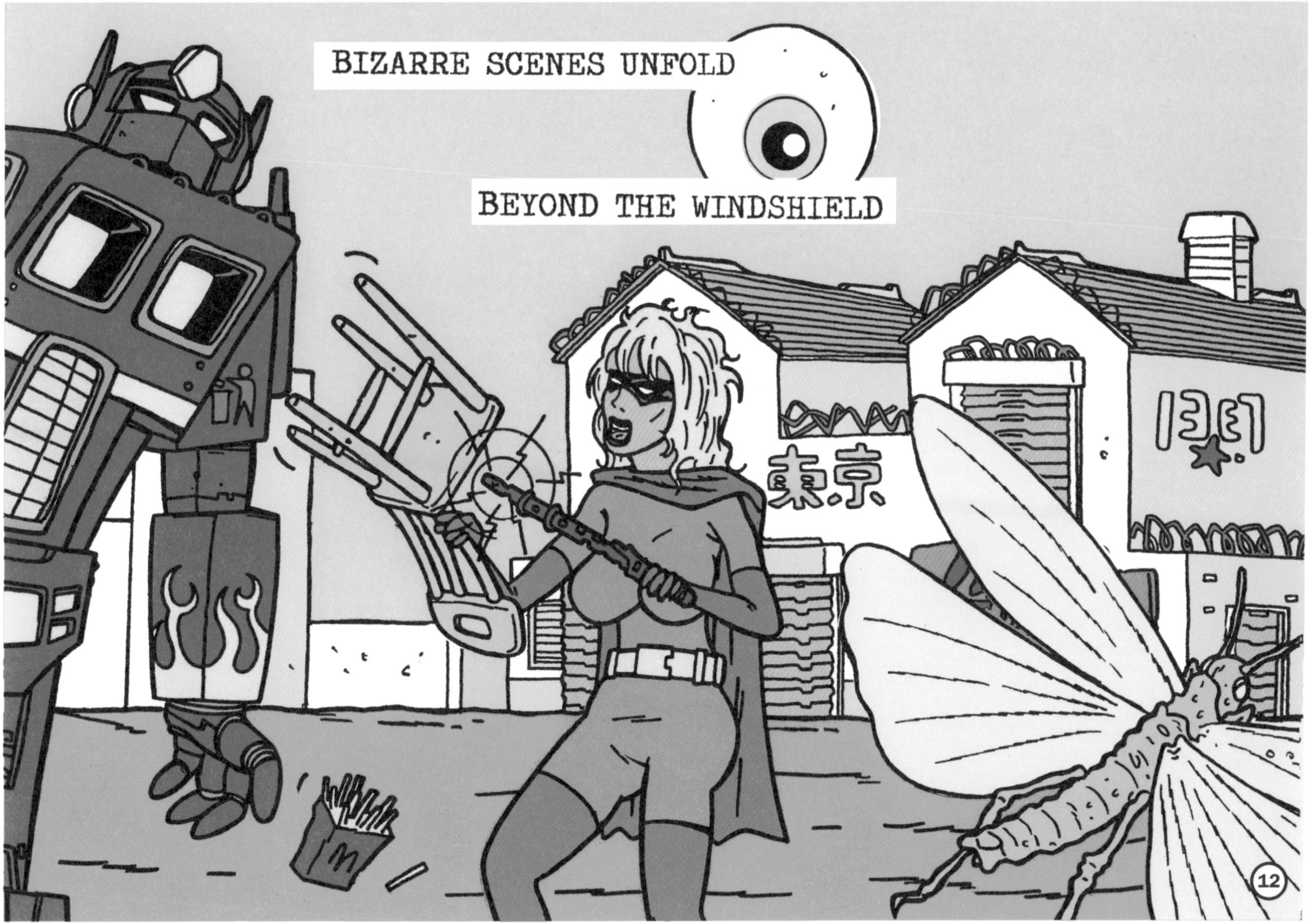
BIZARRE SCENES UNFOLD
BEYOND THE WINDSHIELD
東京

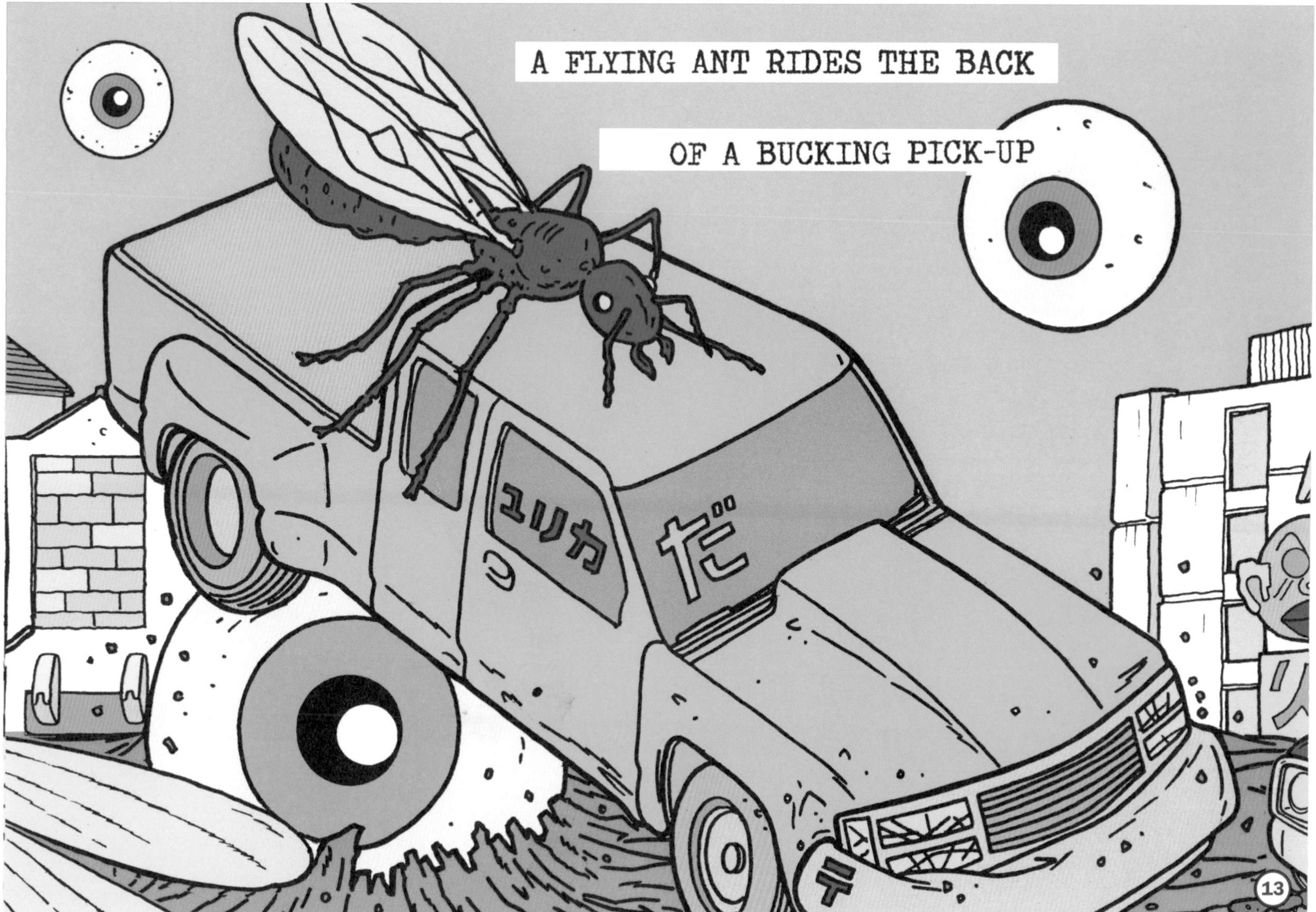
A FLYING ANT RIDES THE BACK
OF A BUCKING PICK-UP
ユリカ
だ

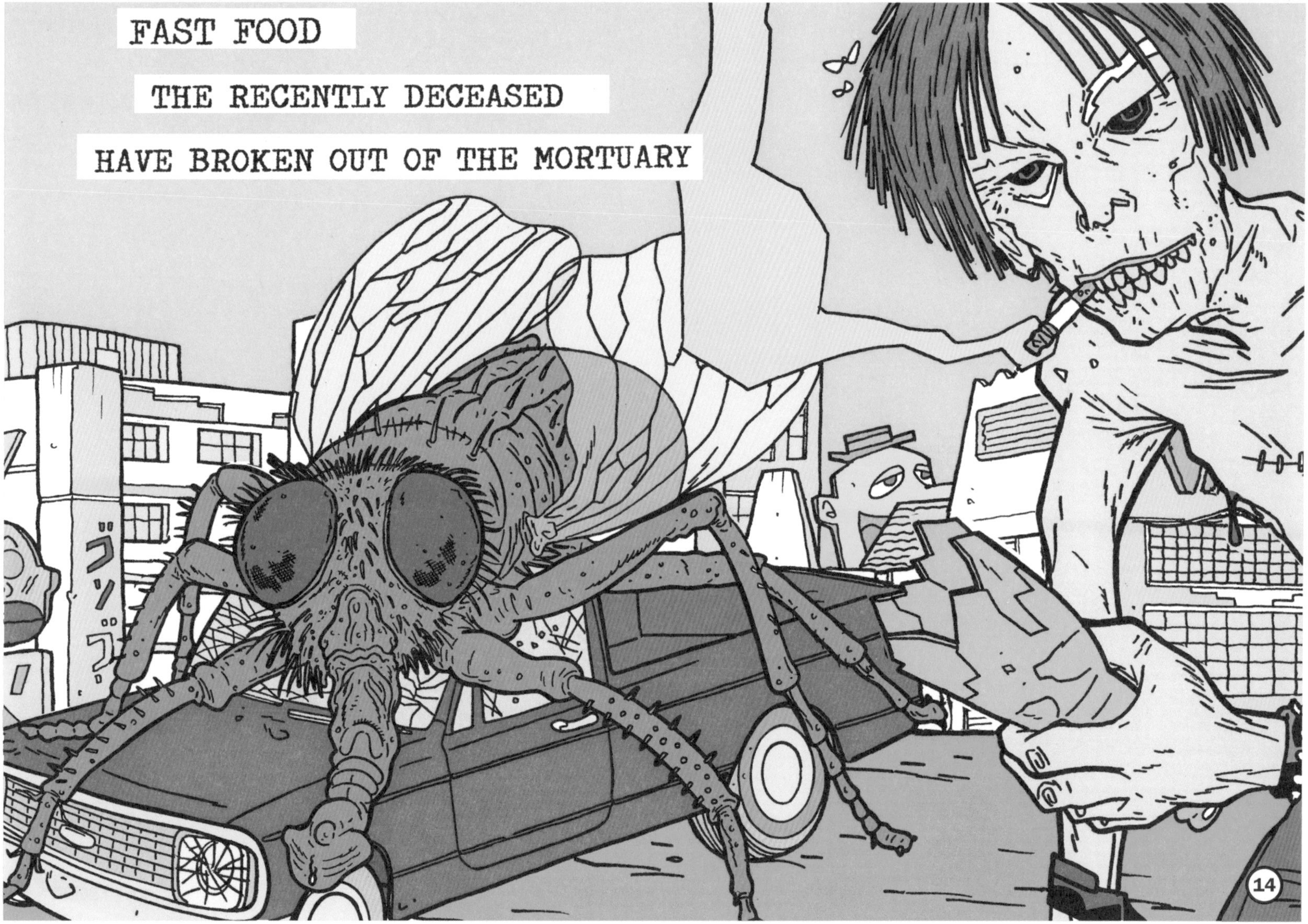
FAST FOOD
THE RECENTLY DECEASED
HAVE BROKEN OUT OF THE MORTUARY

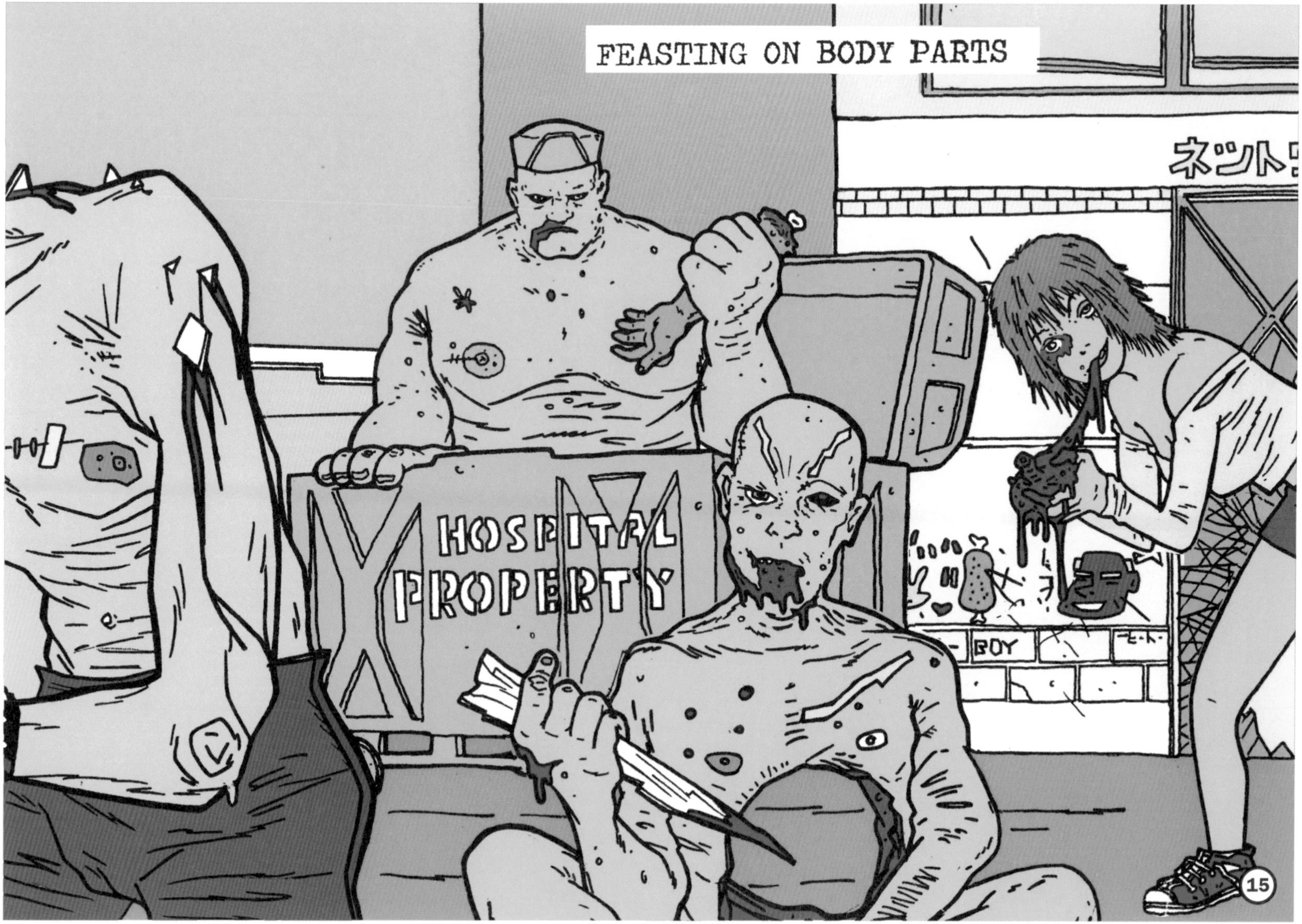
FEASTING ON BODY PARTS
HOSPITAL
PROPERTY
BOY

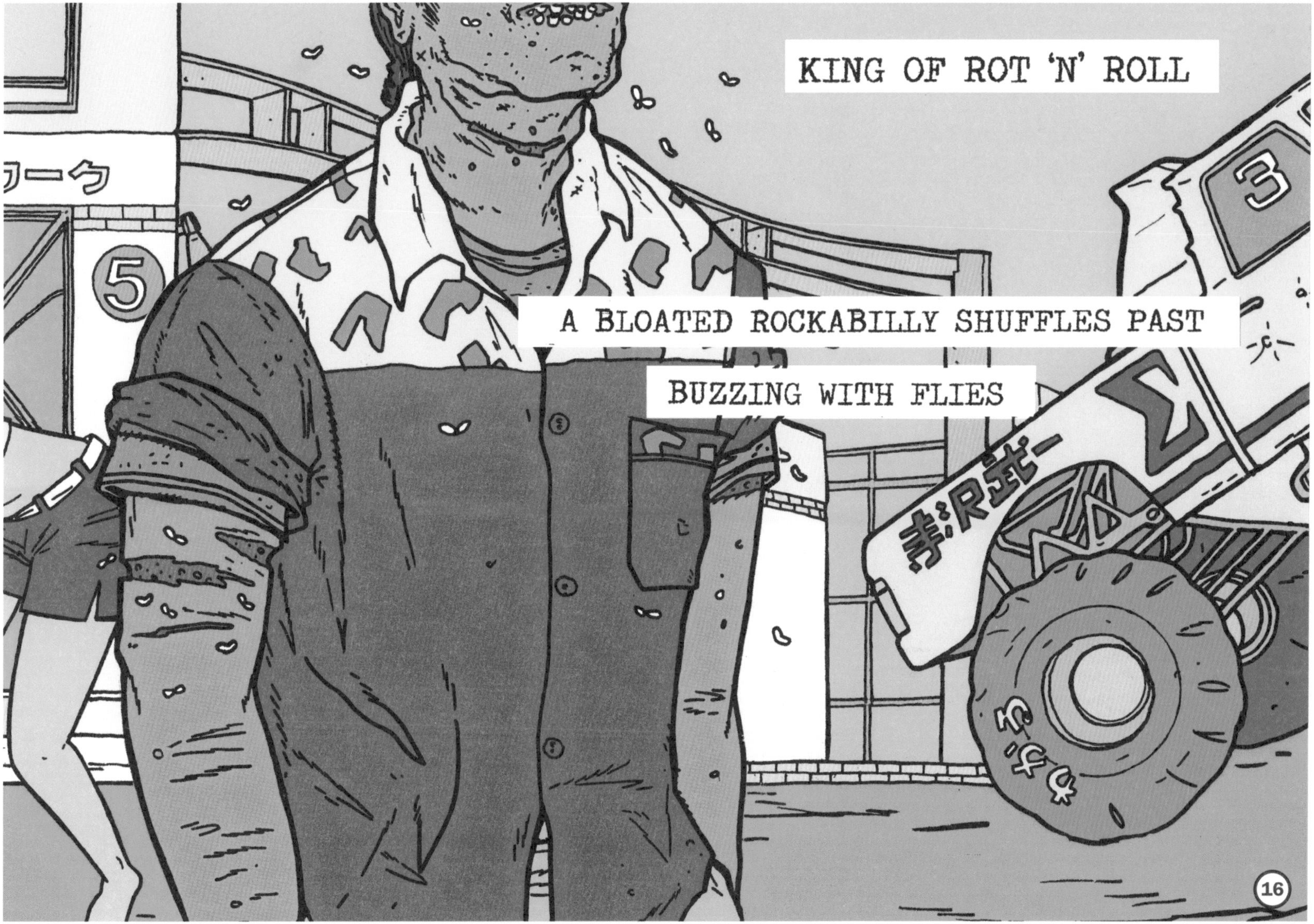
KING OF ROT 'N' ROLL
A BLOATED ROCKABILLY SHUFFLES PAST
BUZZING WITH FLIES

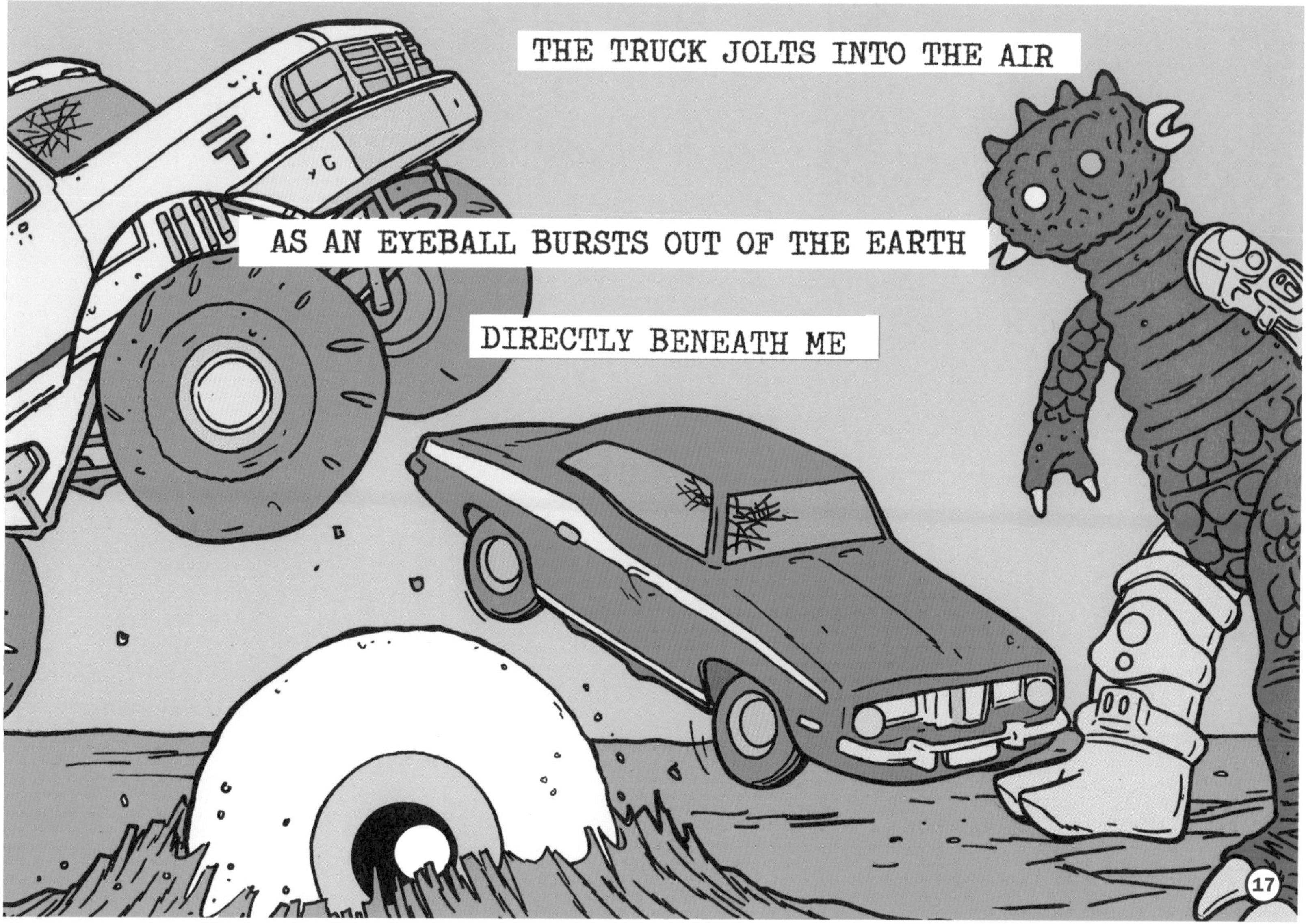
THE TRUCK JOLTS INTO THE AIR
AS AN EYEBALL BURSTS OUT OF THE EARTH
DIRECTLY BENEATH ME

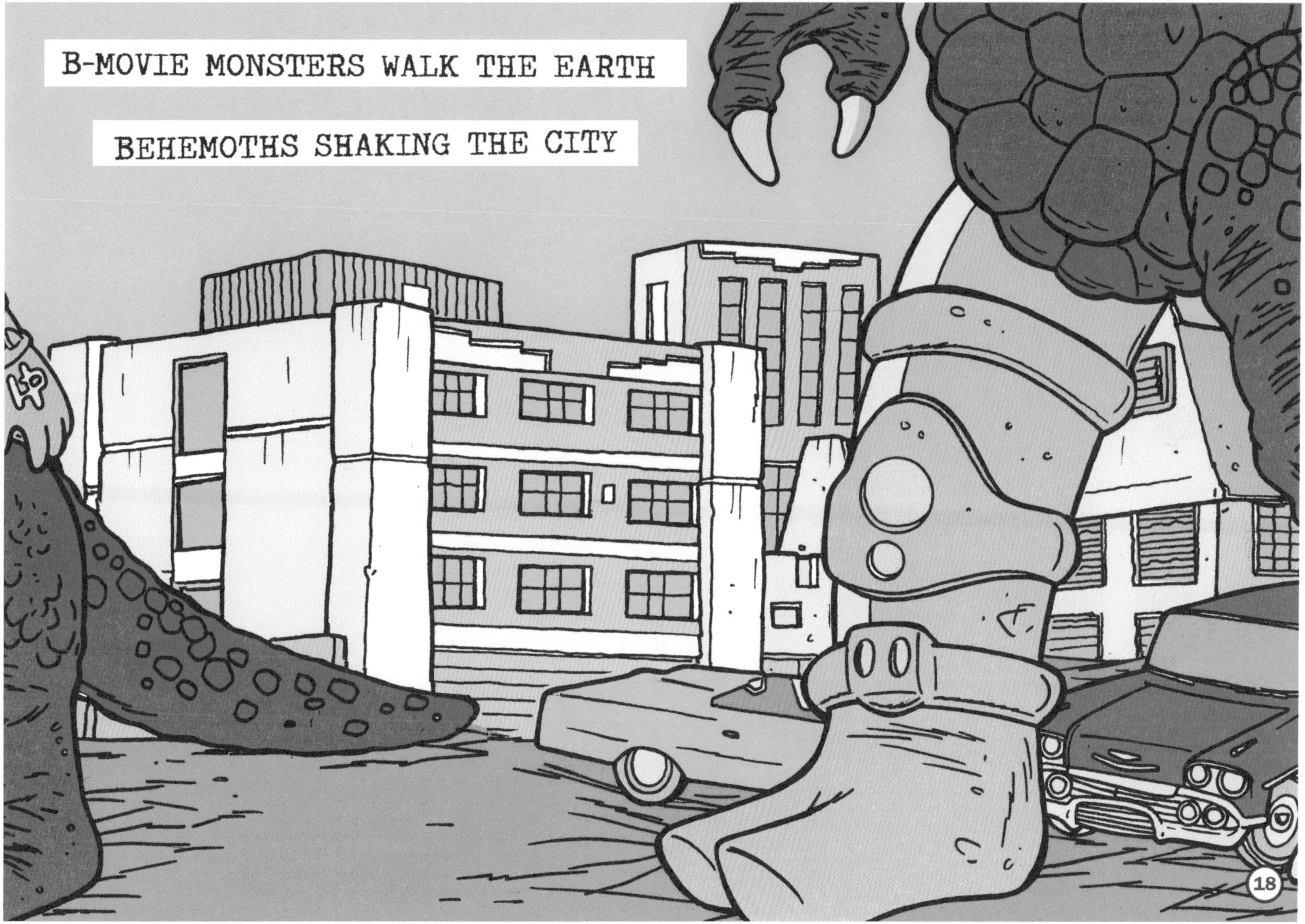
B-MOVIE MONSTERS WALK THE EARTH
BEHEMOTHS SHAKING THE CITY

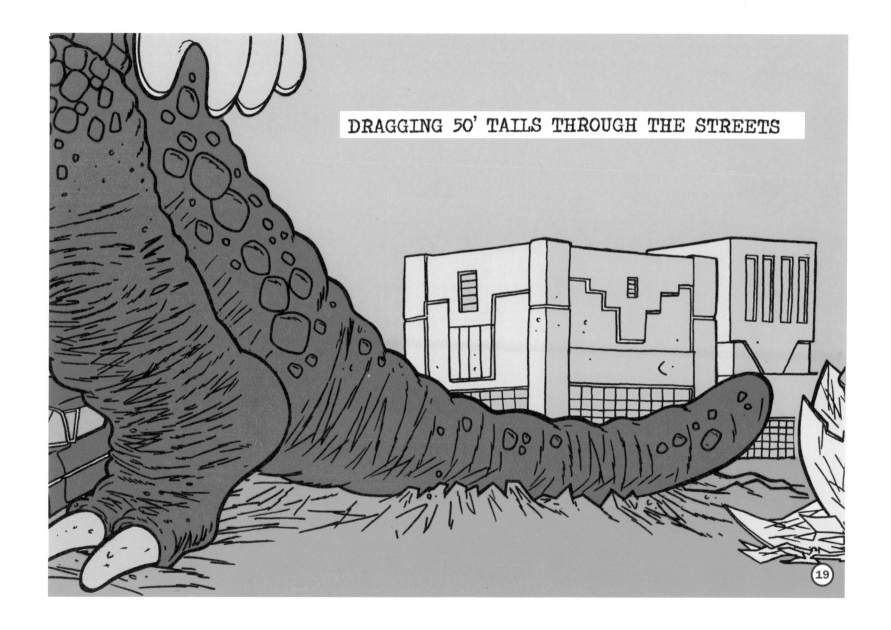

DRAGGING 50' TAILS THROUGH THE STREETS

19

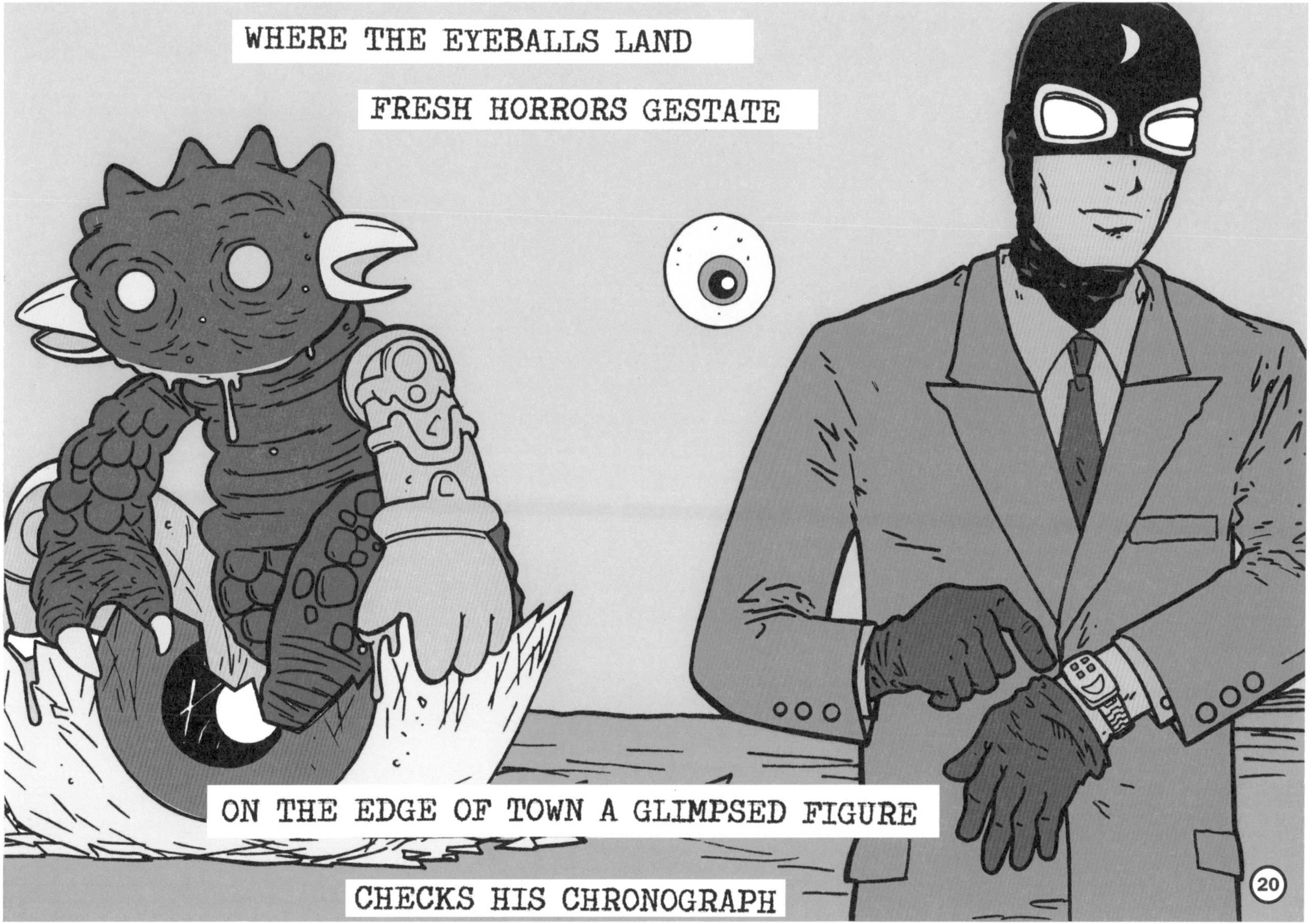
WHERE THE EYEBALLS LAND
FRESH HORRORS GESTATE
ON THE EDGE OF TOWN A GLIMPSED FIGURE
CHECKS HIS CHRONOGRAPH

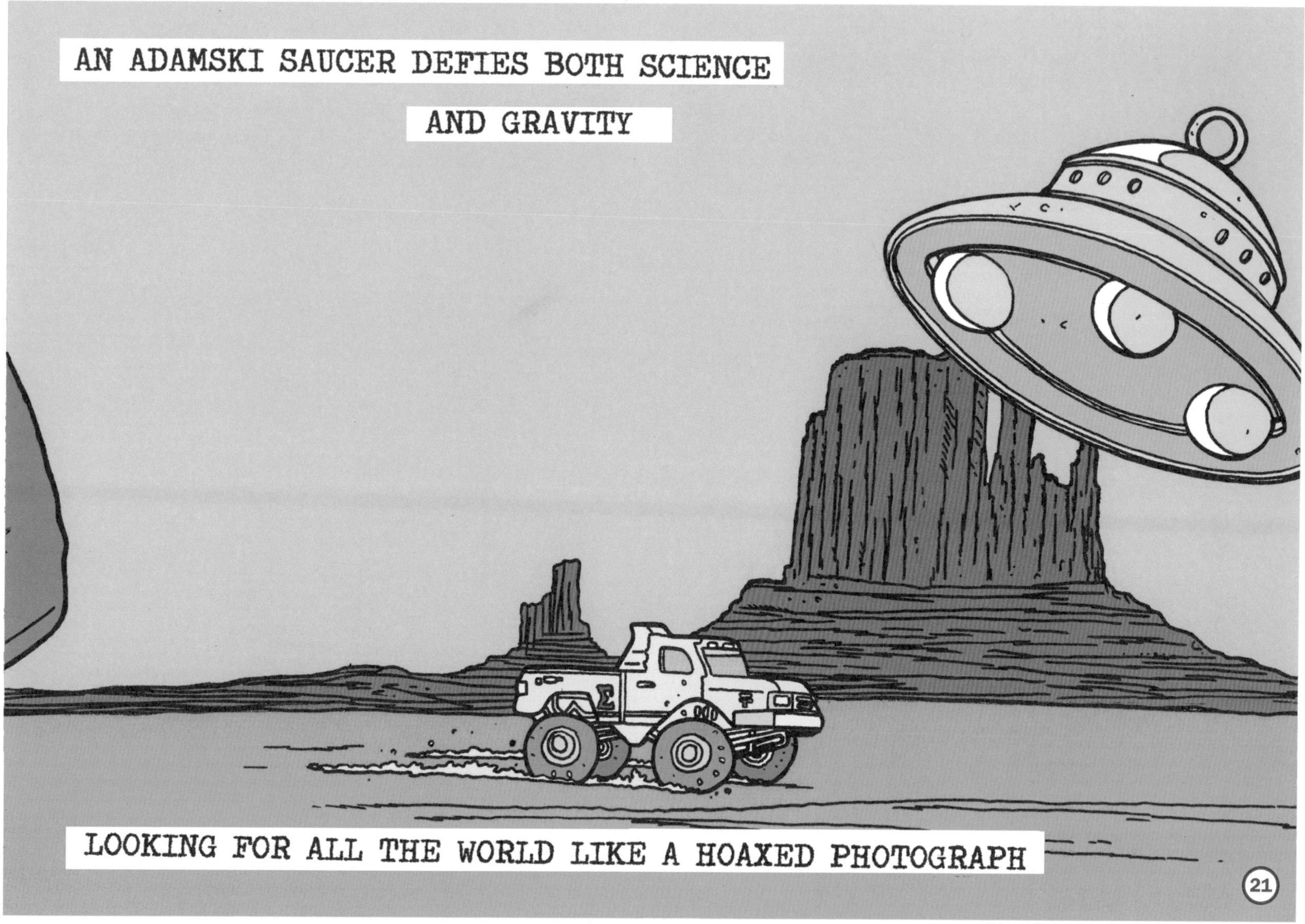
AN ADAMSKI SAUCER DEFIES BOTH SCIENCE
AND GRAVITY
LOOKING FOR ALL THE WORLD LIKE A HOAXED PHOTOGRAPH

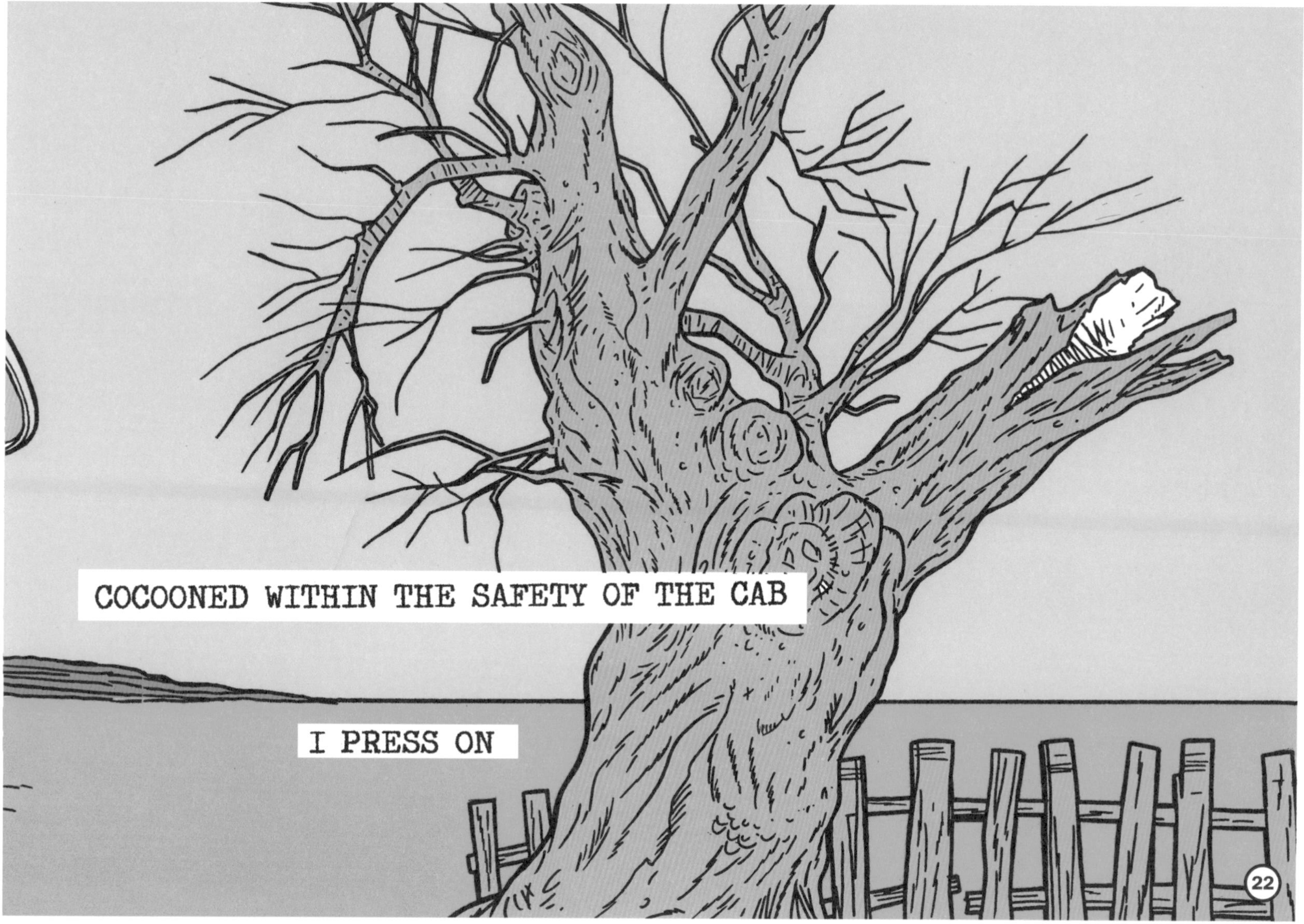
COCOONED WITHIN THE SAFETY OF THE CAB
I PRESS ON

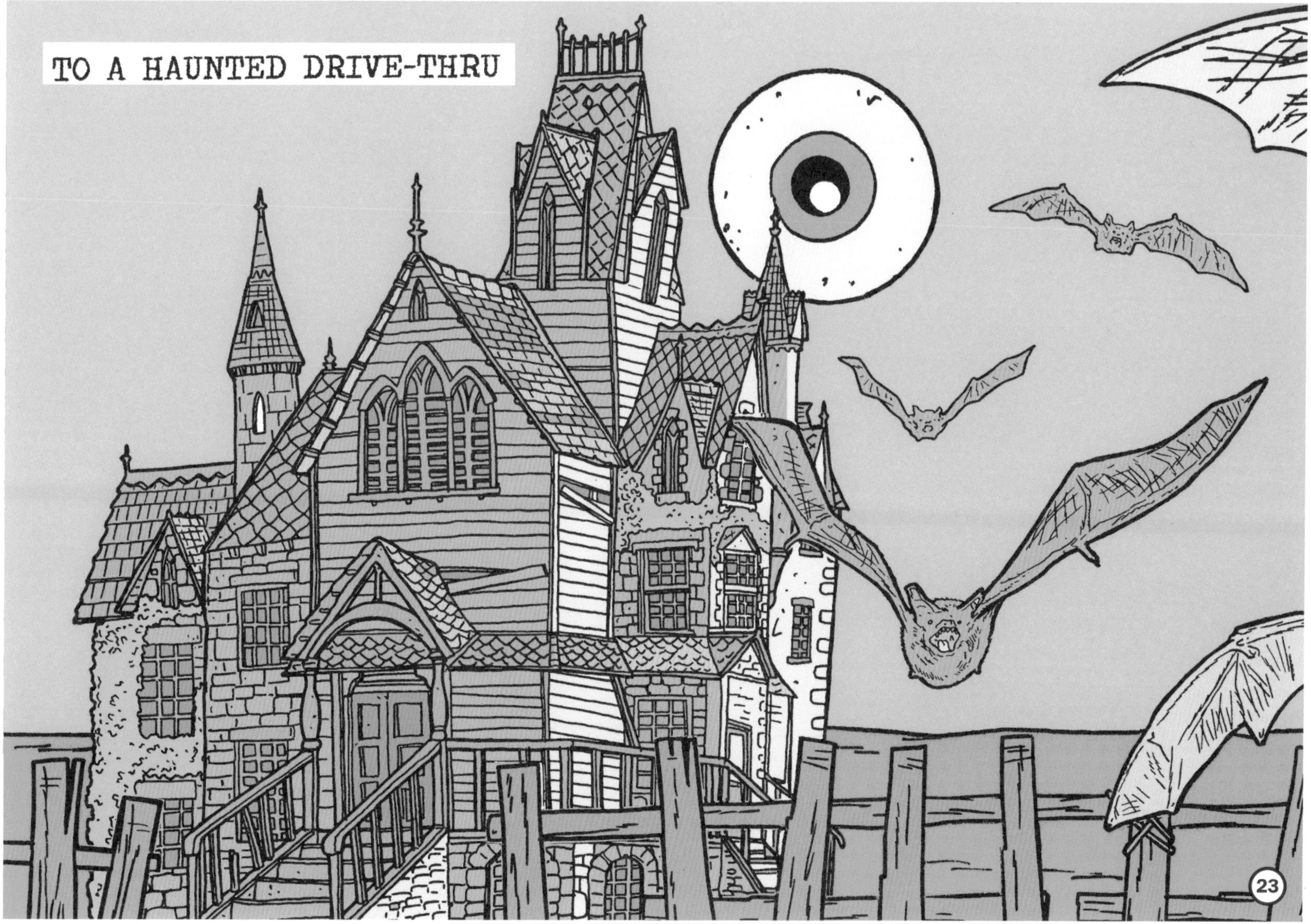
TO A HAUNTED DRIVE-THRU

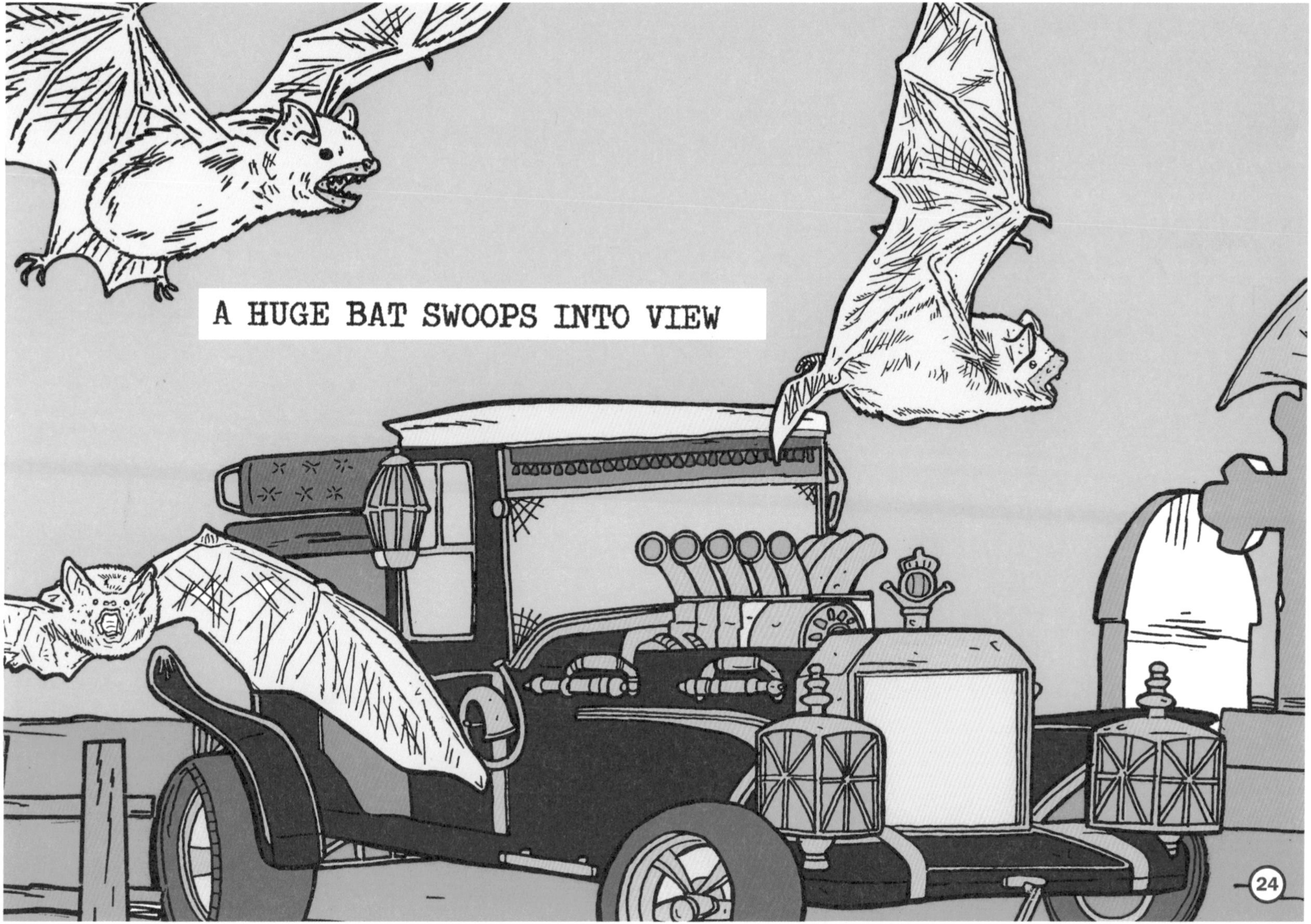
A HUGE BAT SWOOPS INTO VIEW
24

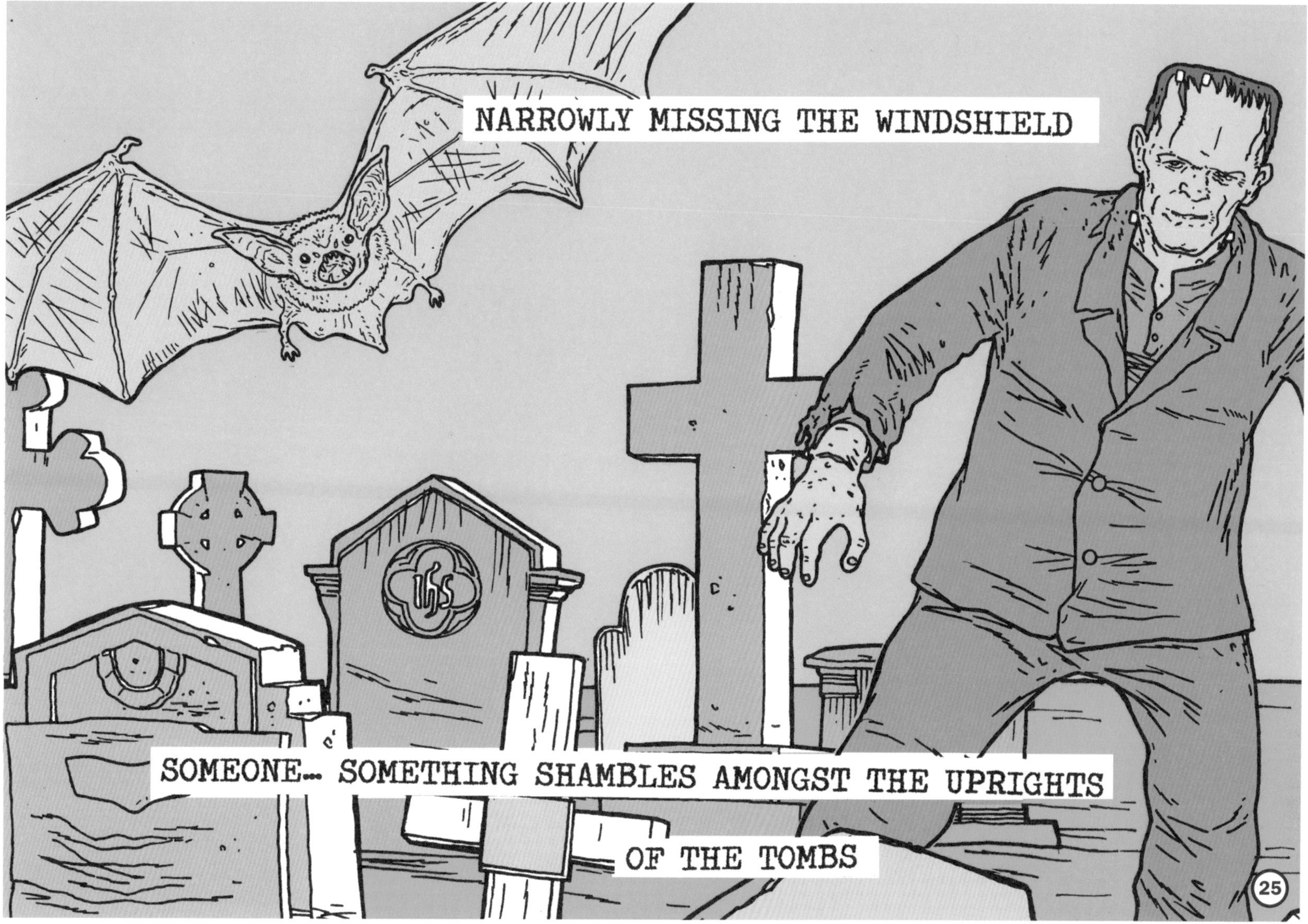
NARROWLY MISSING THE WINDSHIELD
SOMEONE... SOMETHING SHAMBLES AMONGST THE UPRIGHTS
OF THE TOMBS

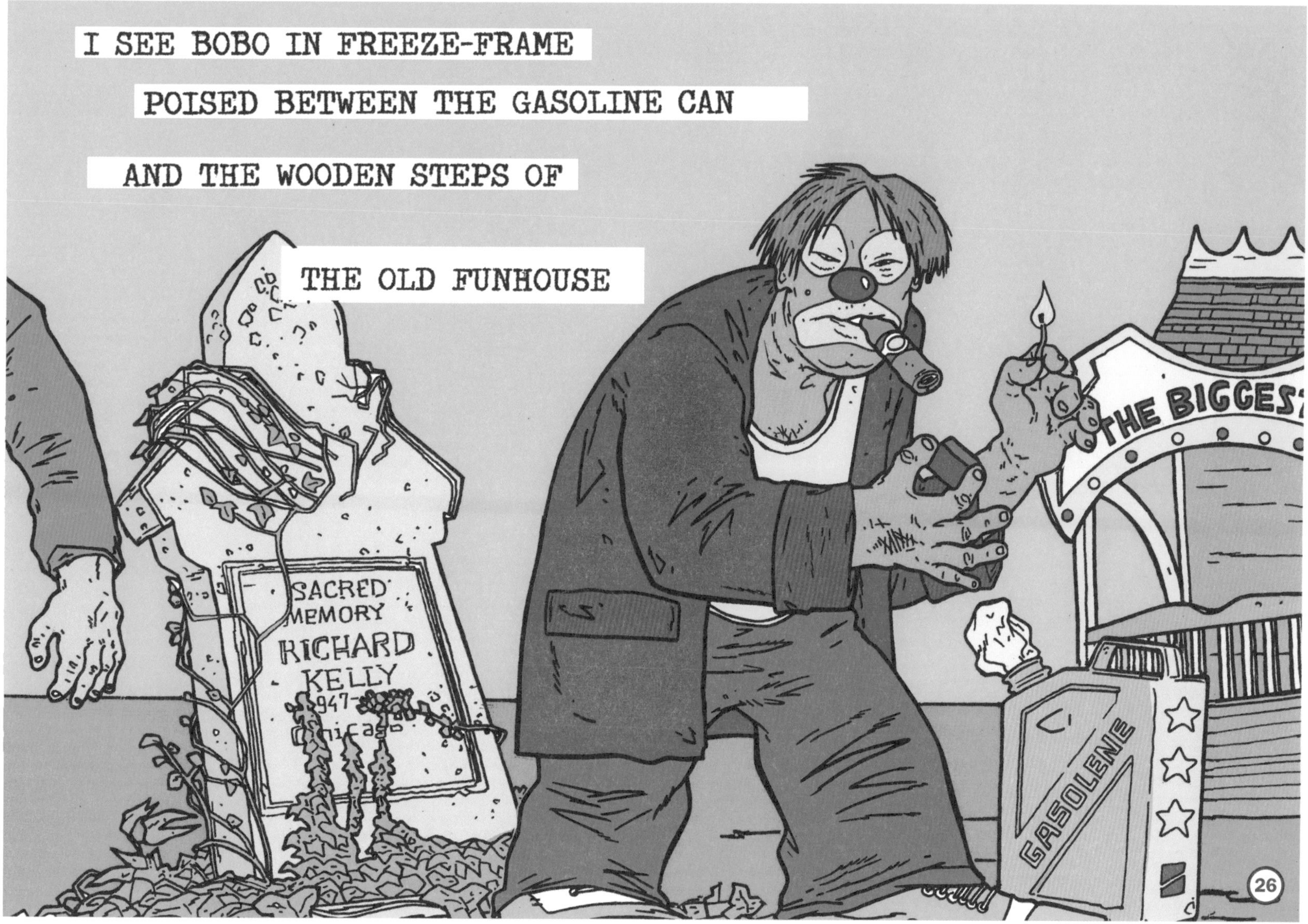
I SEE BOBO IN FREEZE-FRAME
POISED BETWEEN THE GASOLINE CAN
AND THE WOODEN STEPS OF
THE OLD FUNHOUSE
SACRED MEMORY RICHARD KELLY
THE BIGGEST
GASOLENE

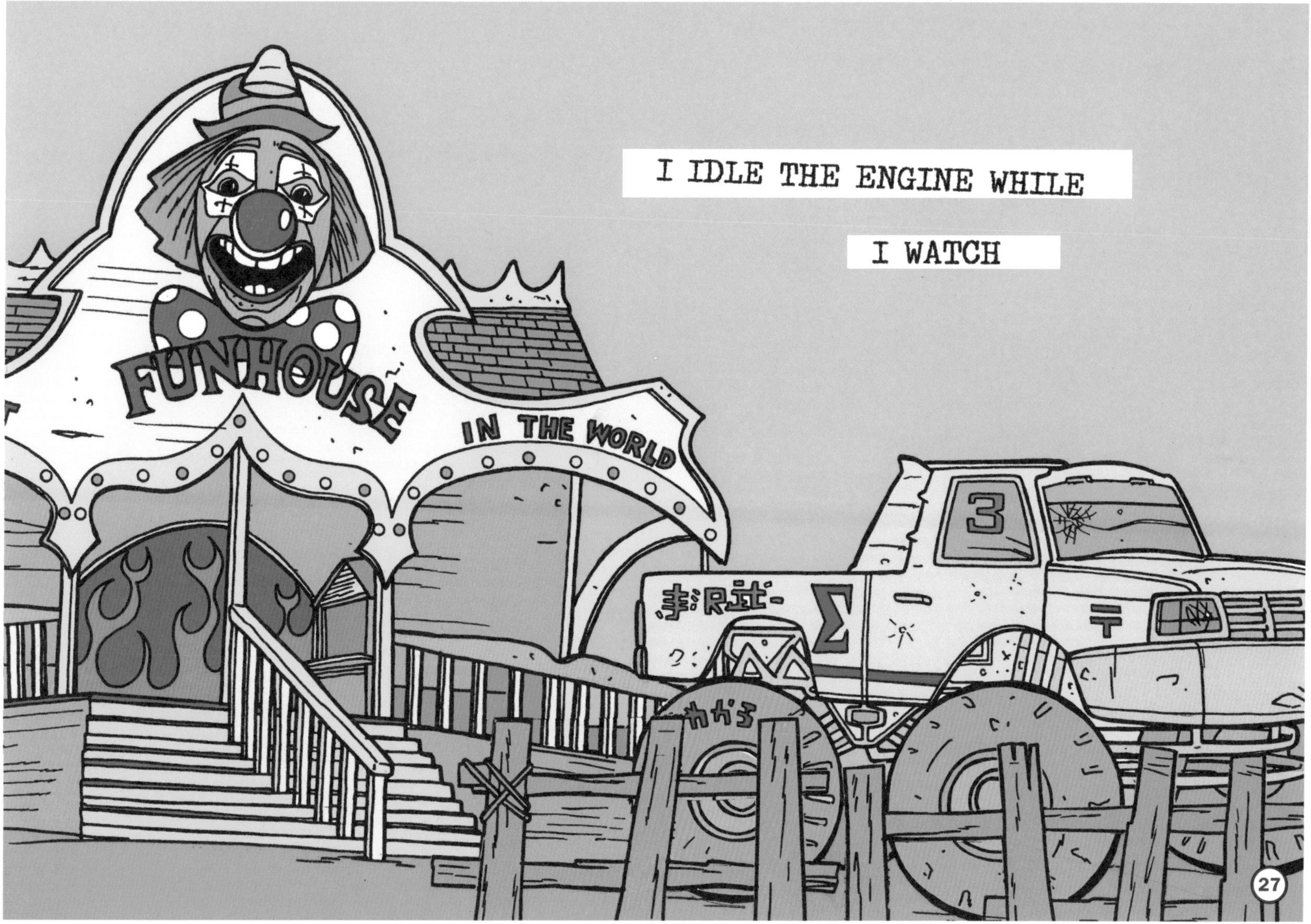
I IDLE THE ENGINE WHILE
I WATCH
FUNHOUSE
IN THE WORLD
3

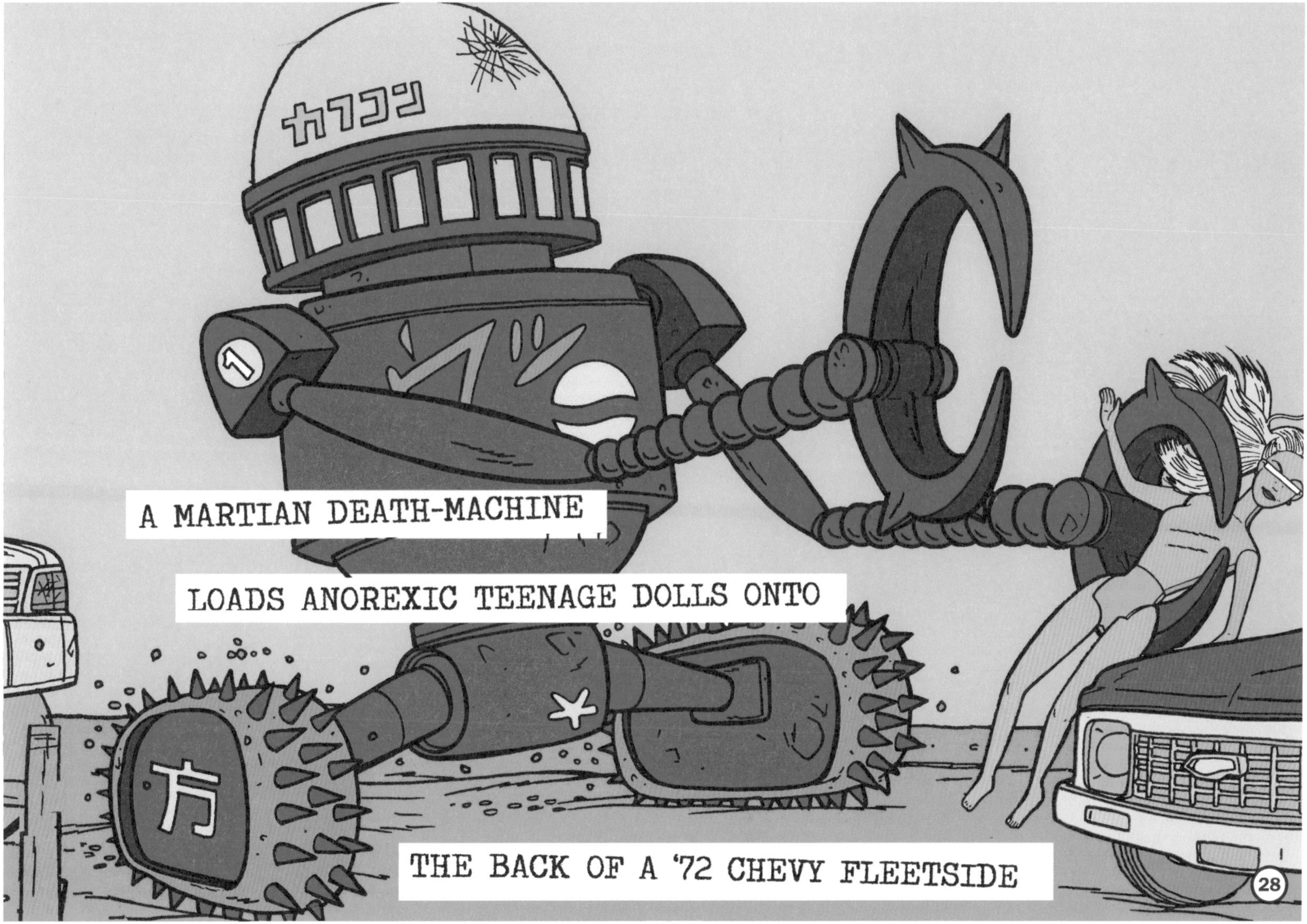
A MARTIAN DEATH-MACHINE
LOADS ANOREXIC TEENAGE DOLLS ONTO
THE BACK OF A '72 CHEVY FLEETSIDE
方

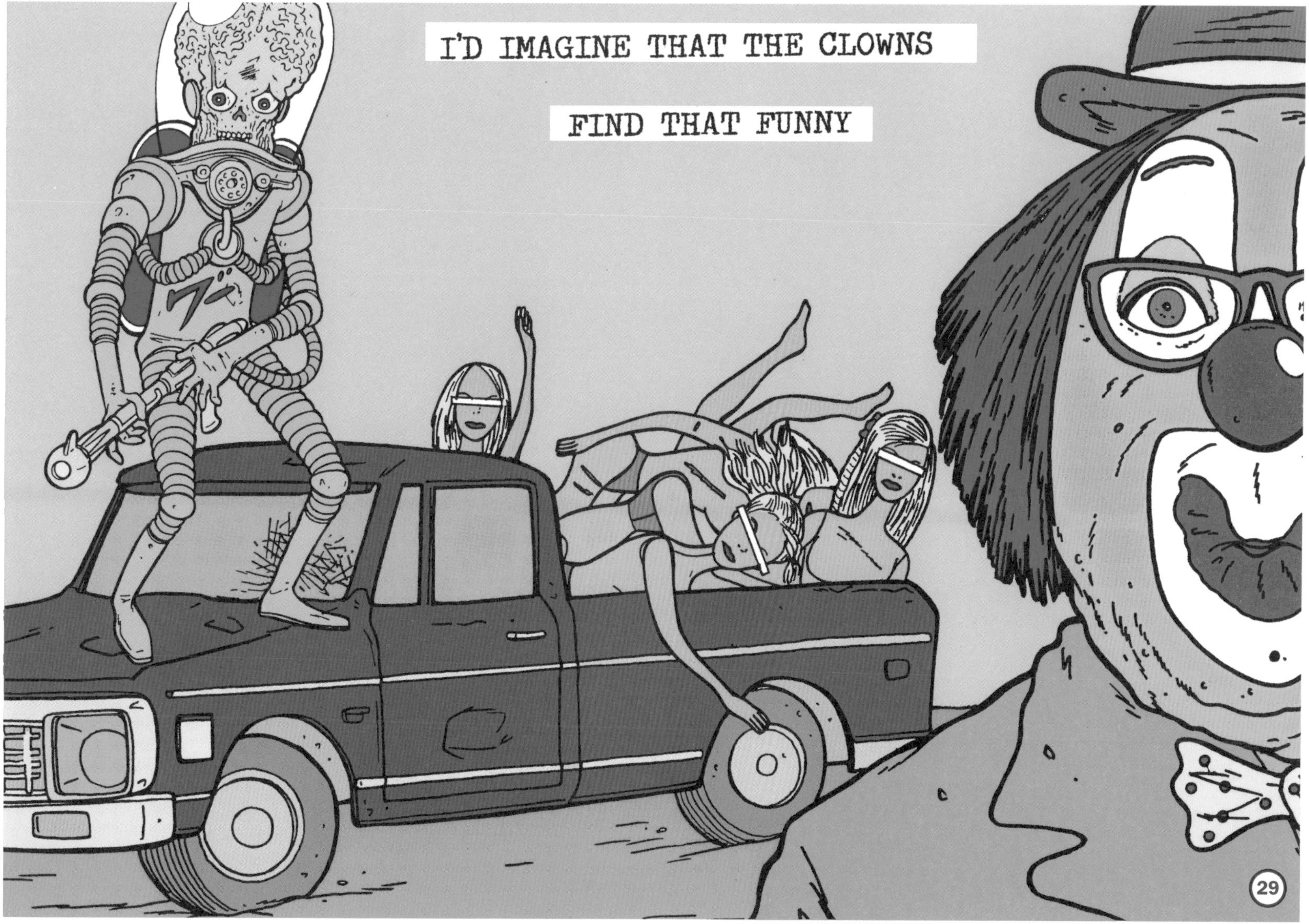
I'D IMAGINE THAT THE CLOWNS
FIND THAT FUNNY

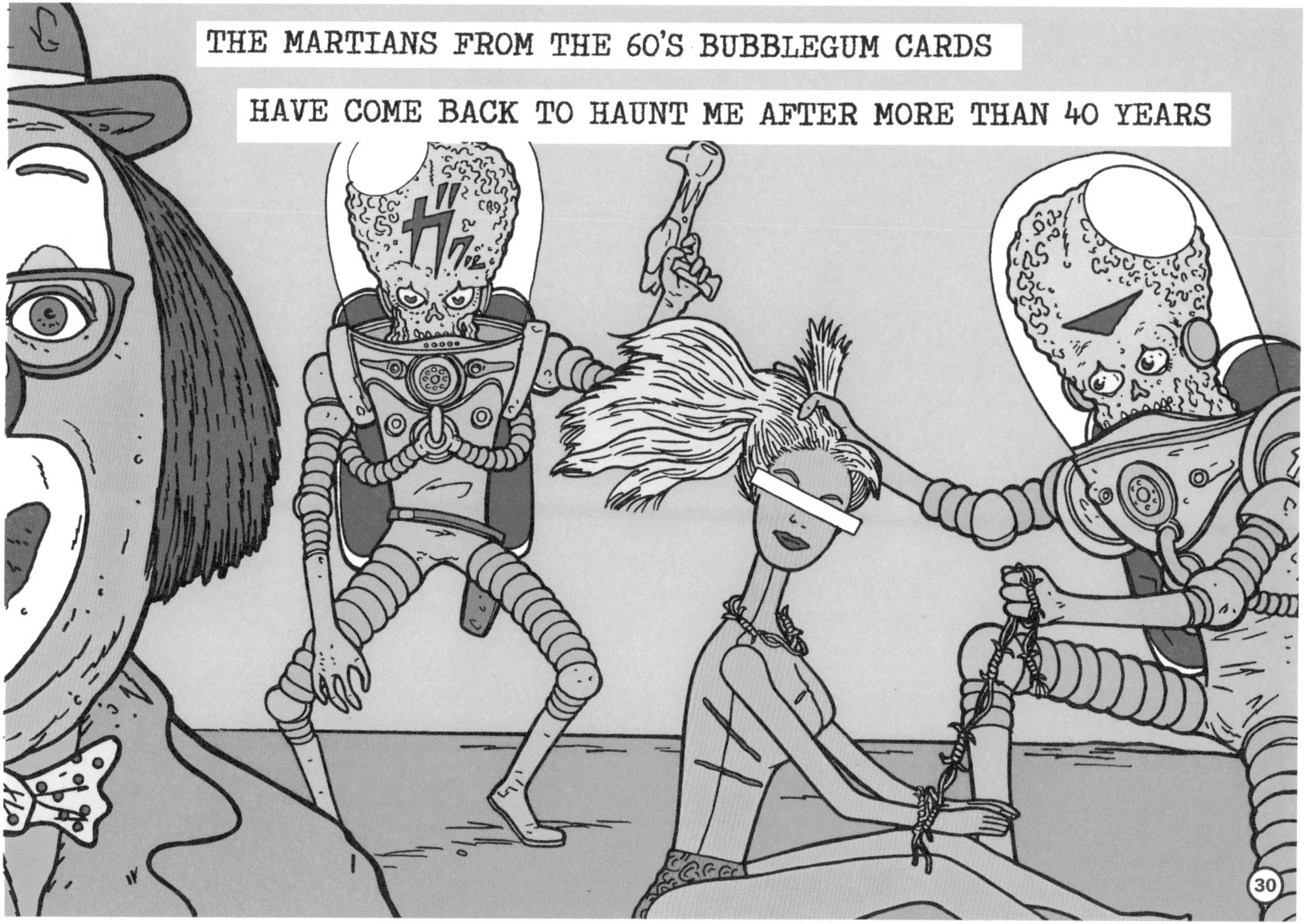
THE MARTIANS FROM THE 60'S BUBBLEGUM CARDS
HAVE COME BACK TO HAUNT ME AFTER MORE THAN 40 YEARS

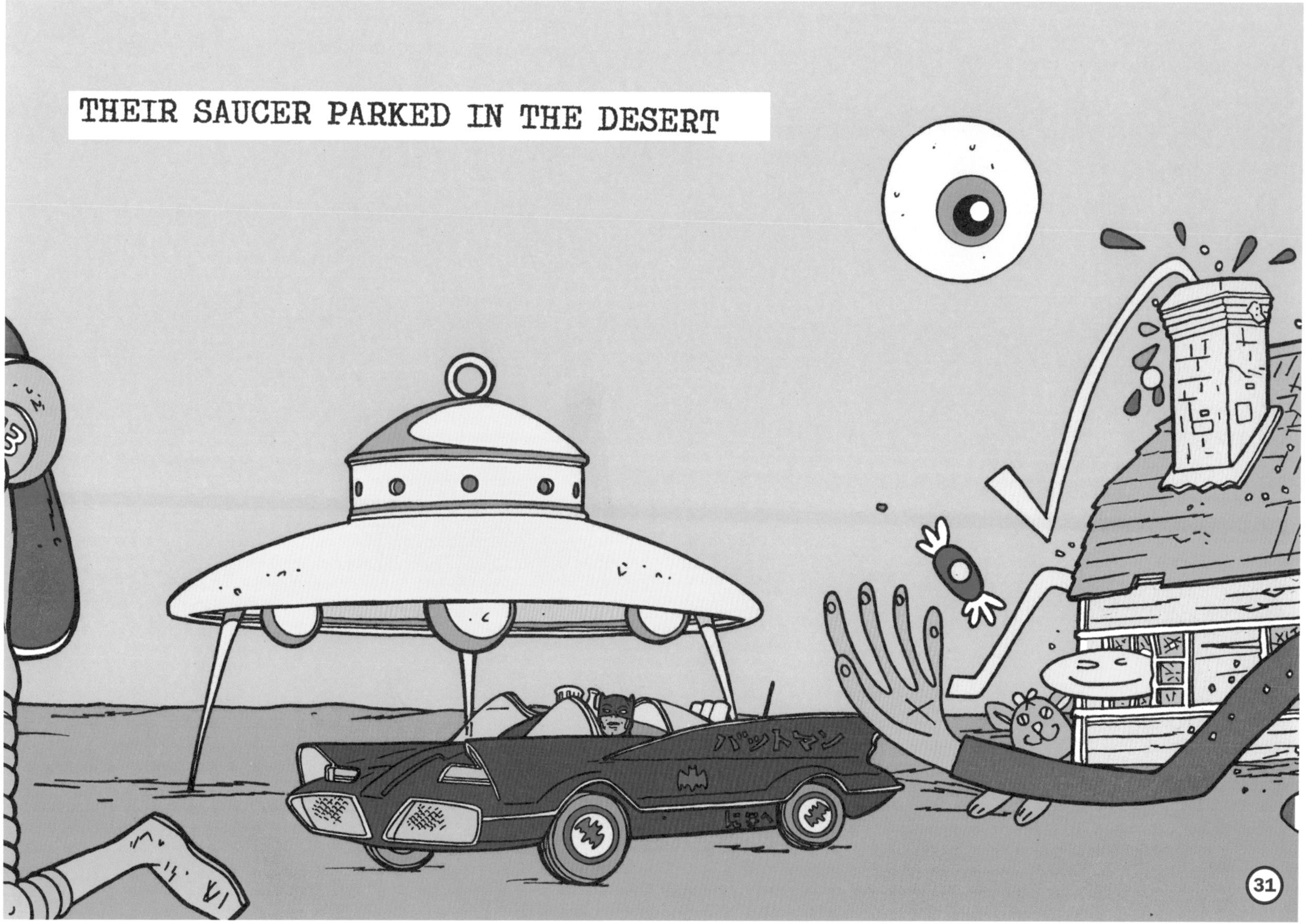
THEIR SAUCER PARKED IN THE DESERT
バットマン

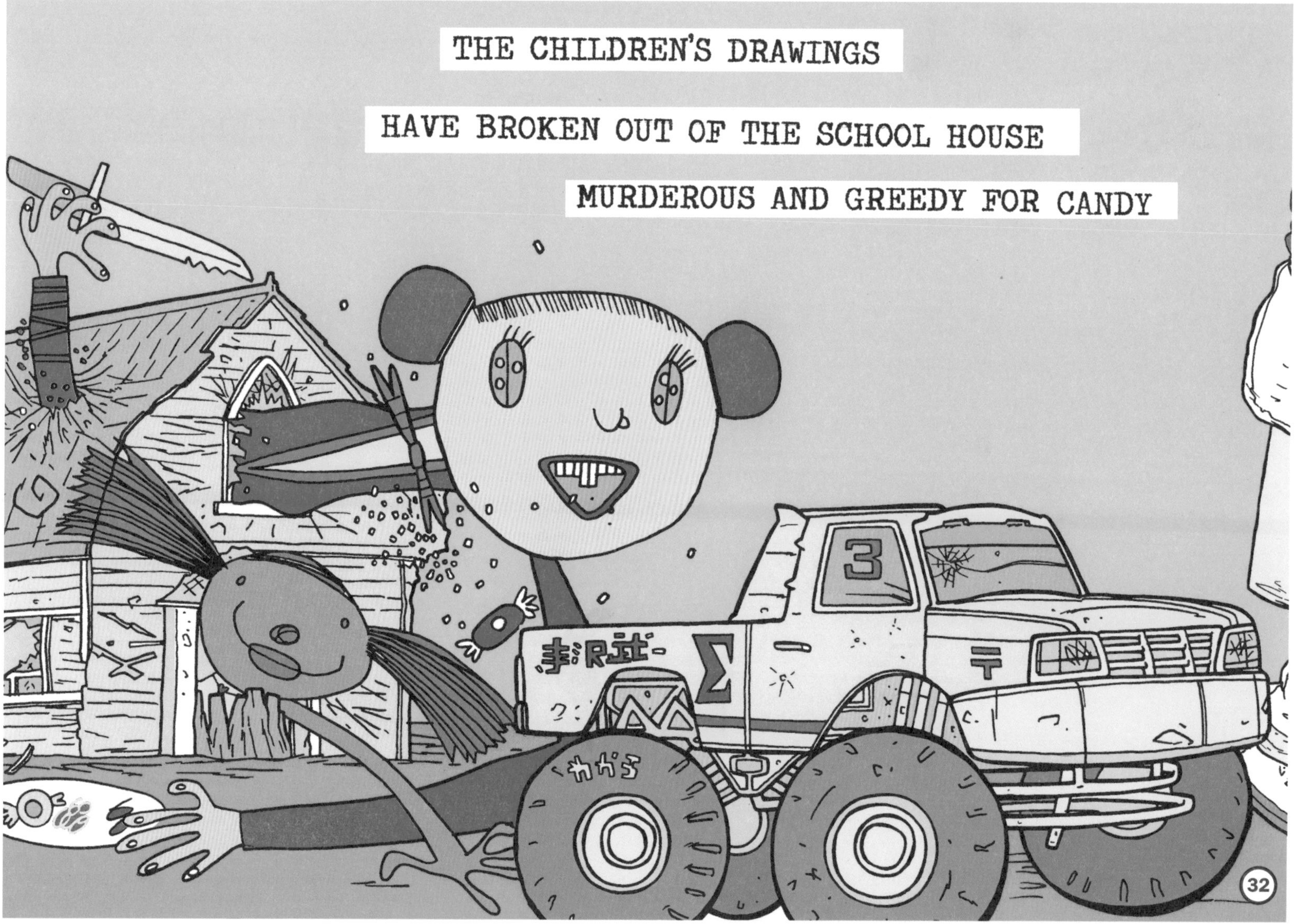
THE CHILDREN'S DRAWINGS
HAVE BROKEN OUT OF THE SCHOOL HOUSE
MURDEROUS AND GREEDY FOR CANDY
3

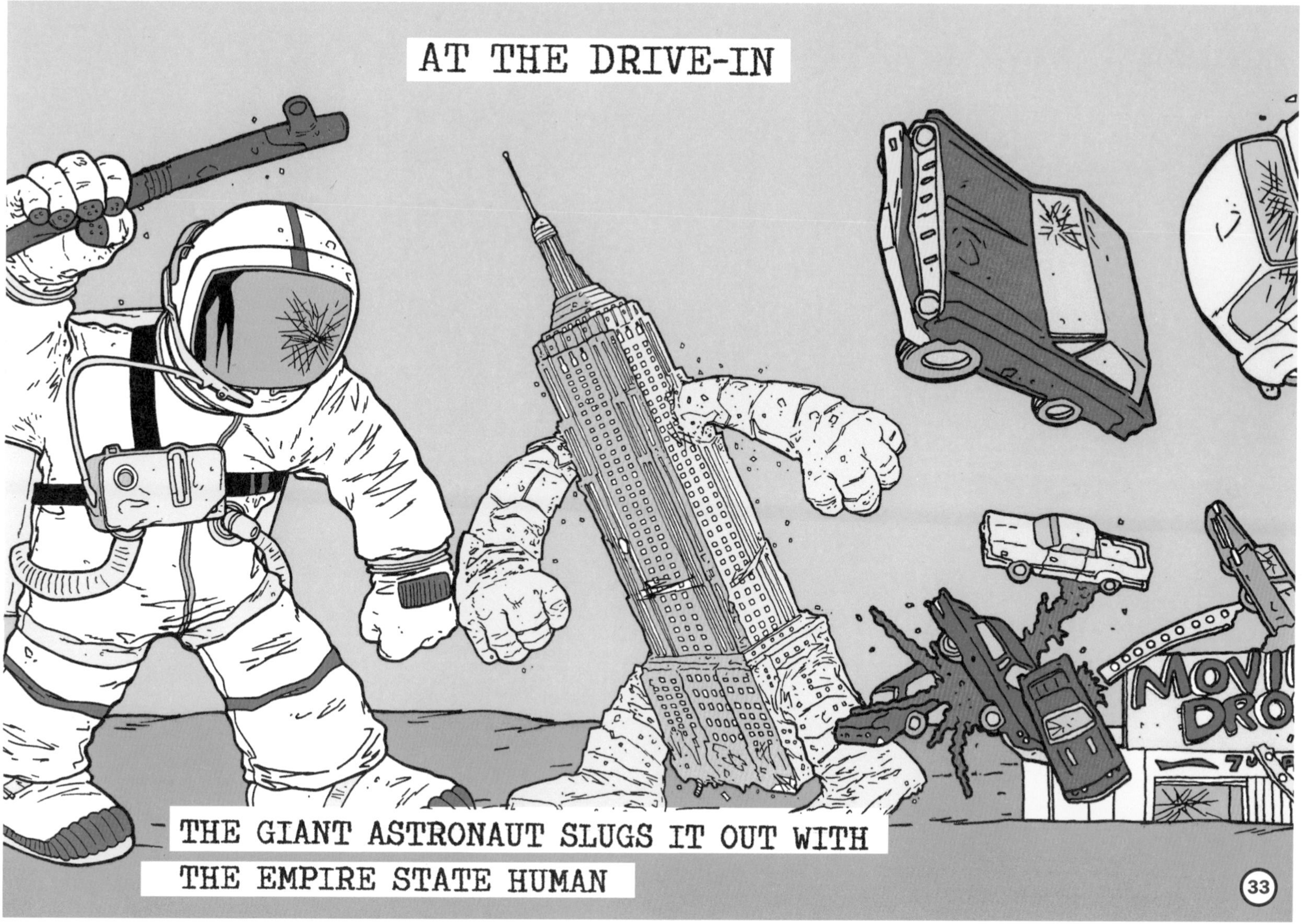
AT THE DRIVE-IN
THE GIANT ASTRONAUT SLUGS IT OUT WITH
THE EMPIRE STATE HUMAN

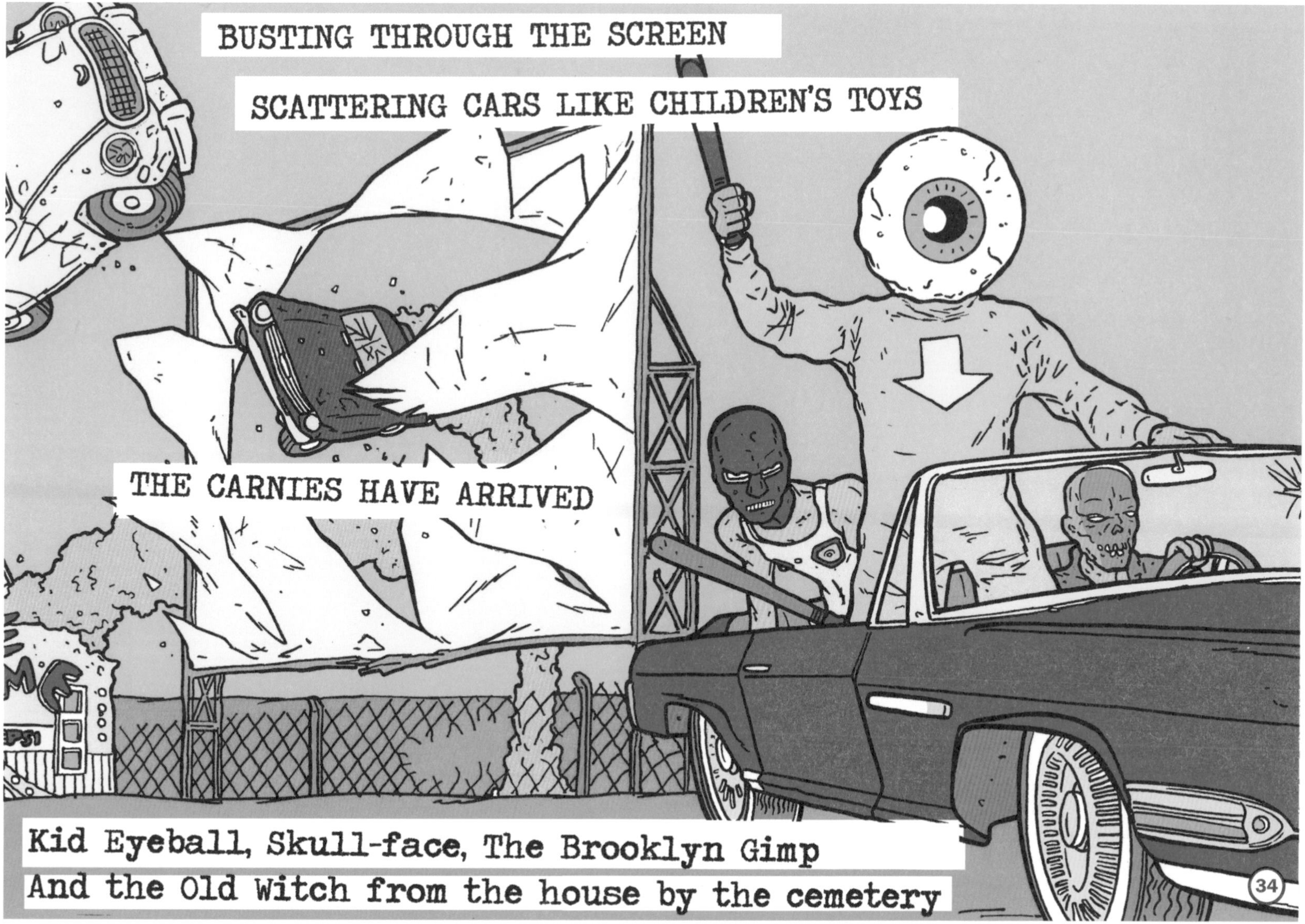
BUSTING THROUGH THE SCREEN
SCATTERING CARS LIKE CHILDREN'S TOYS
THE CARNIES HAVE ARRIVED
Kid Eyeball, Skull-face, The Brooklyn Gimp
And the Old Witch from the house by the cemetery

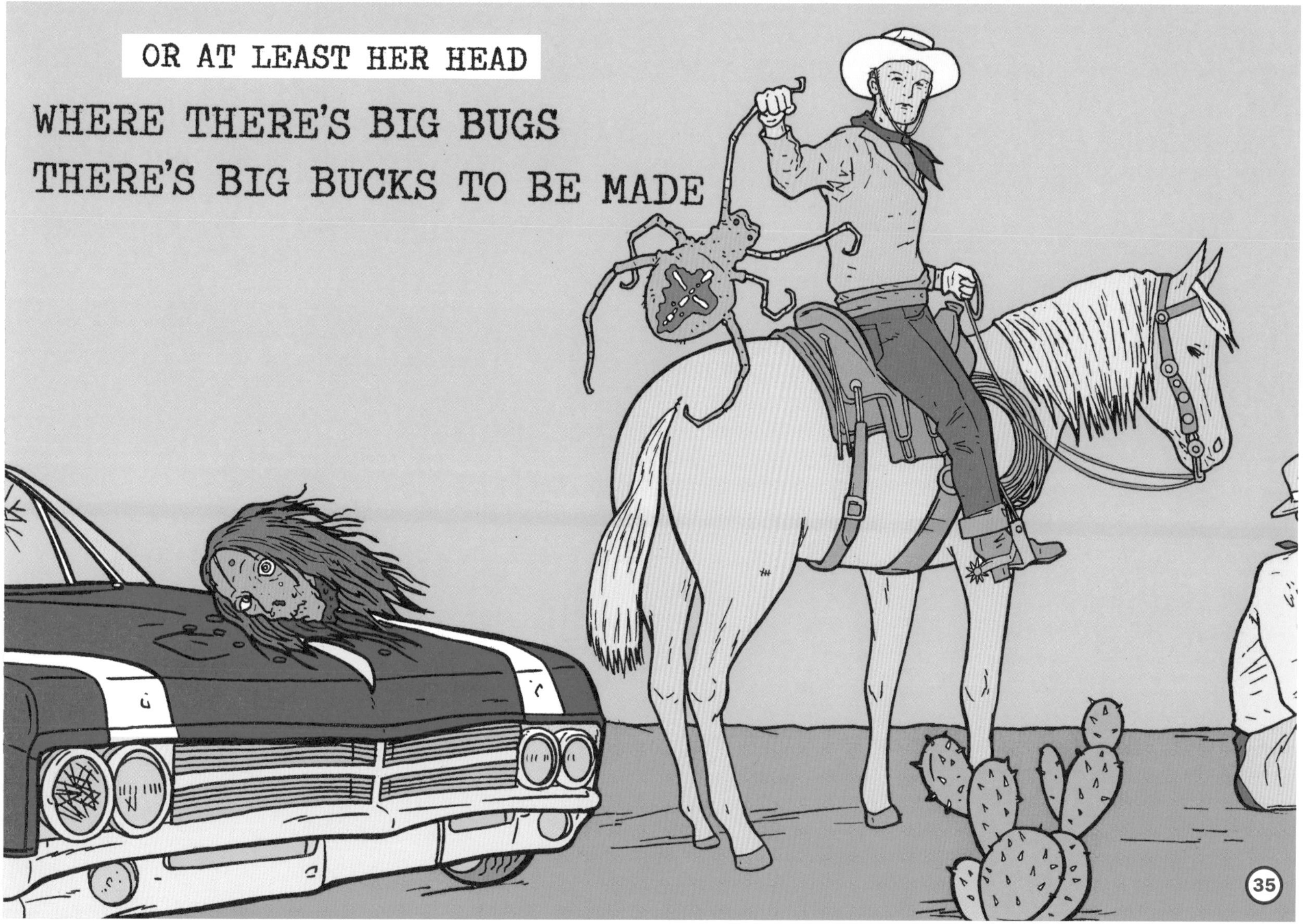
OR AT LEAST HER HEAD
WHERE THERE'S BIG BUGS
THERE'S BIG BUCKS TO BE MADE

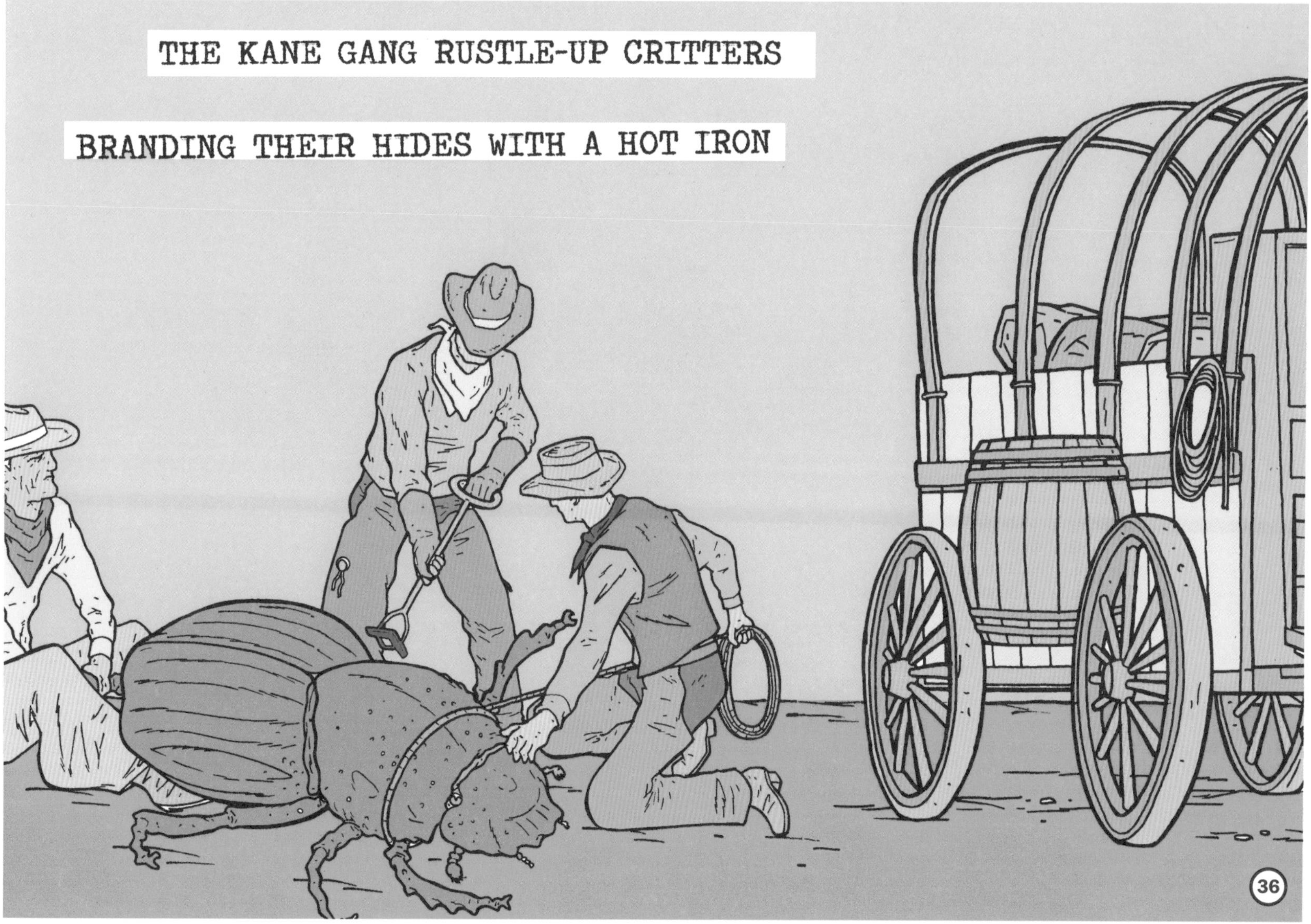
THE KANE GANG RUSTLE-UP CRITTERS
BRANDING THEIR HIDES WITH A HOT IRON

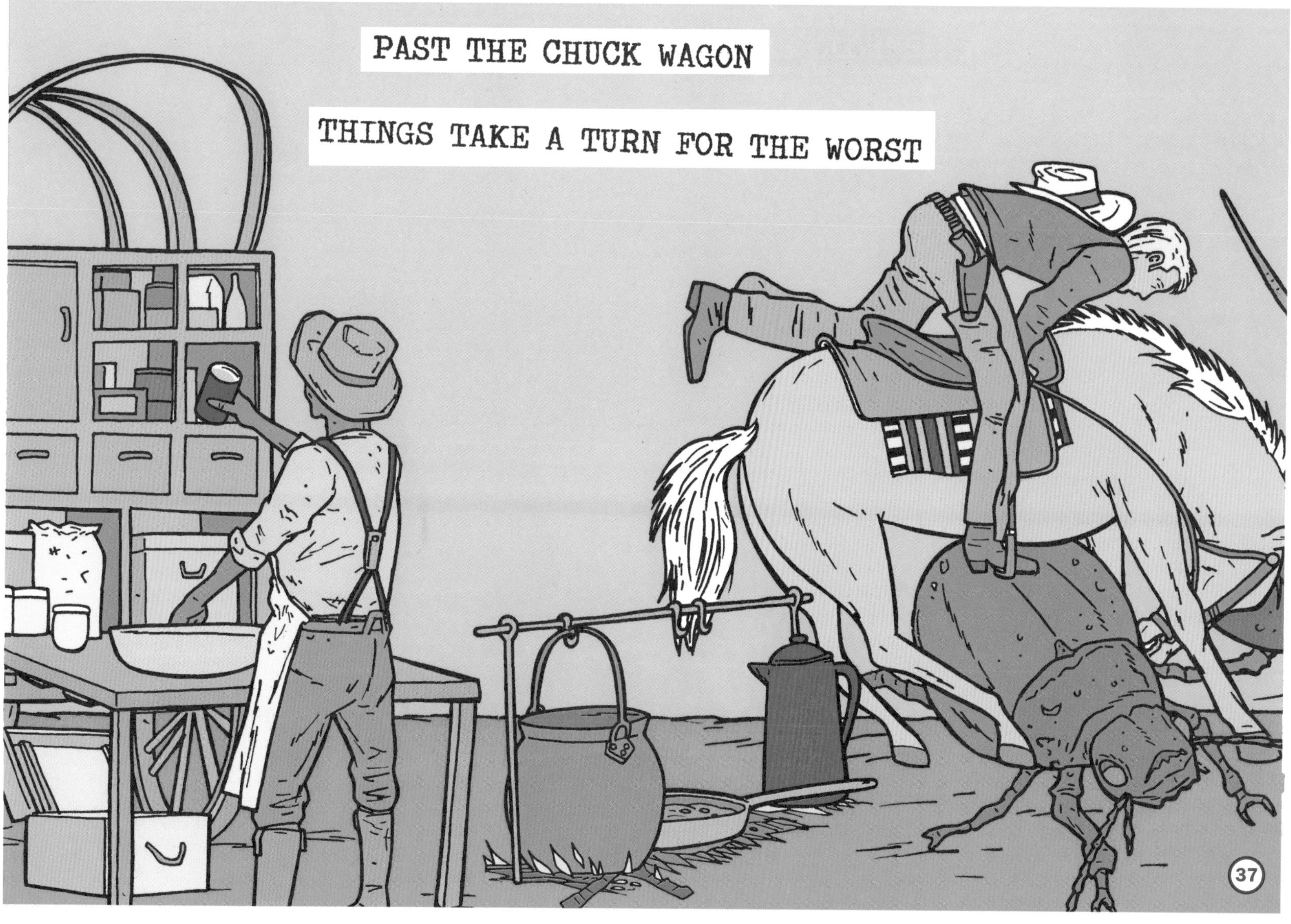
PAST THE CHUCK WAGON
THINGS TAKE A TURN FOR THE WORST

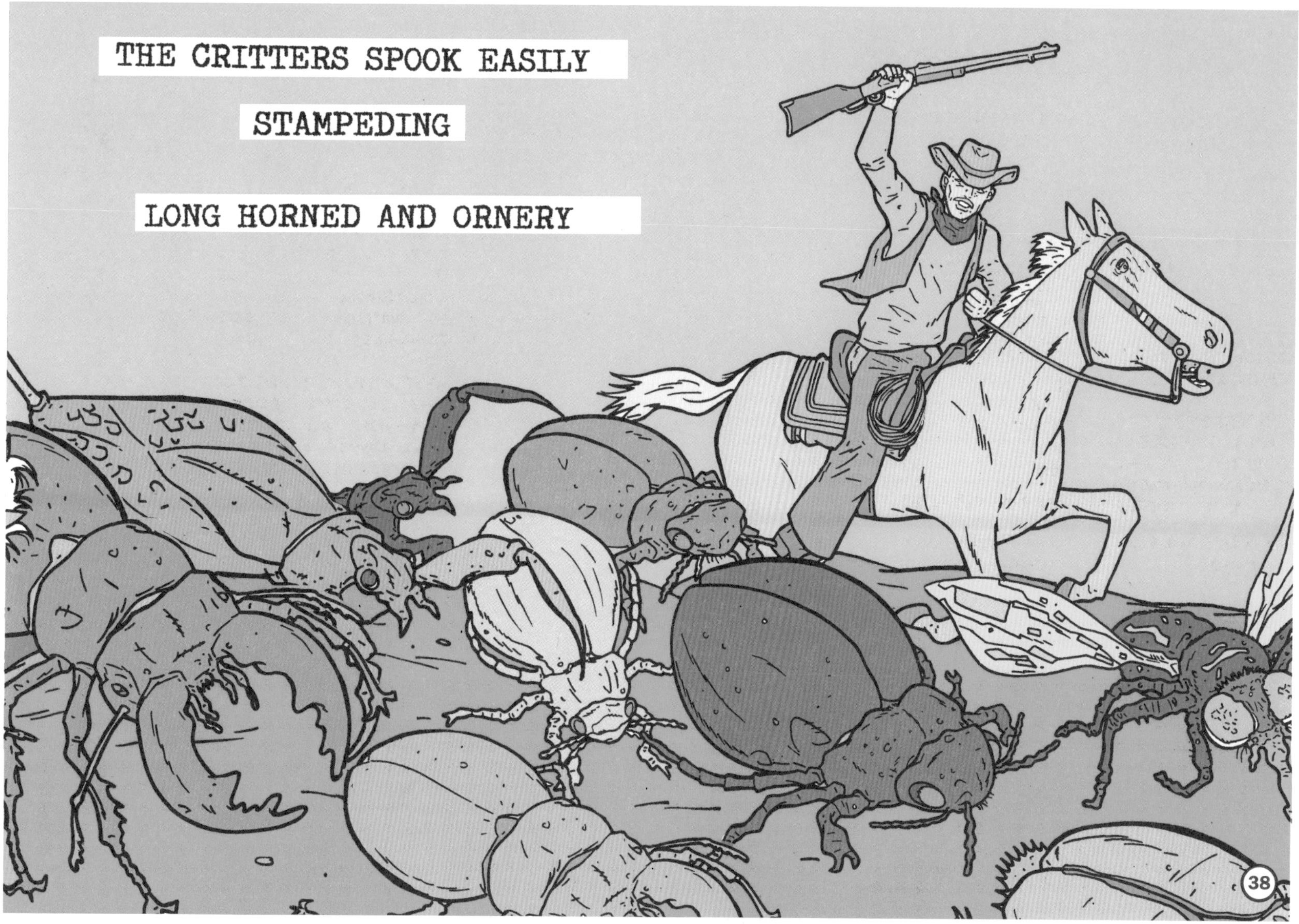
THE CRITTERS SPOOK EASILY
STAMPEDING
LONG HORNED AND ORNERY

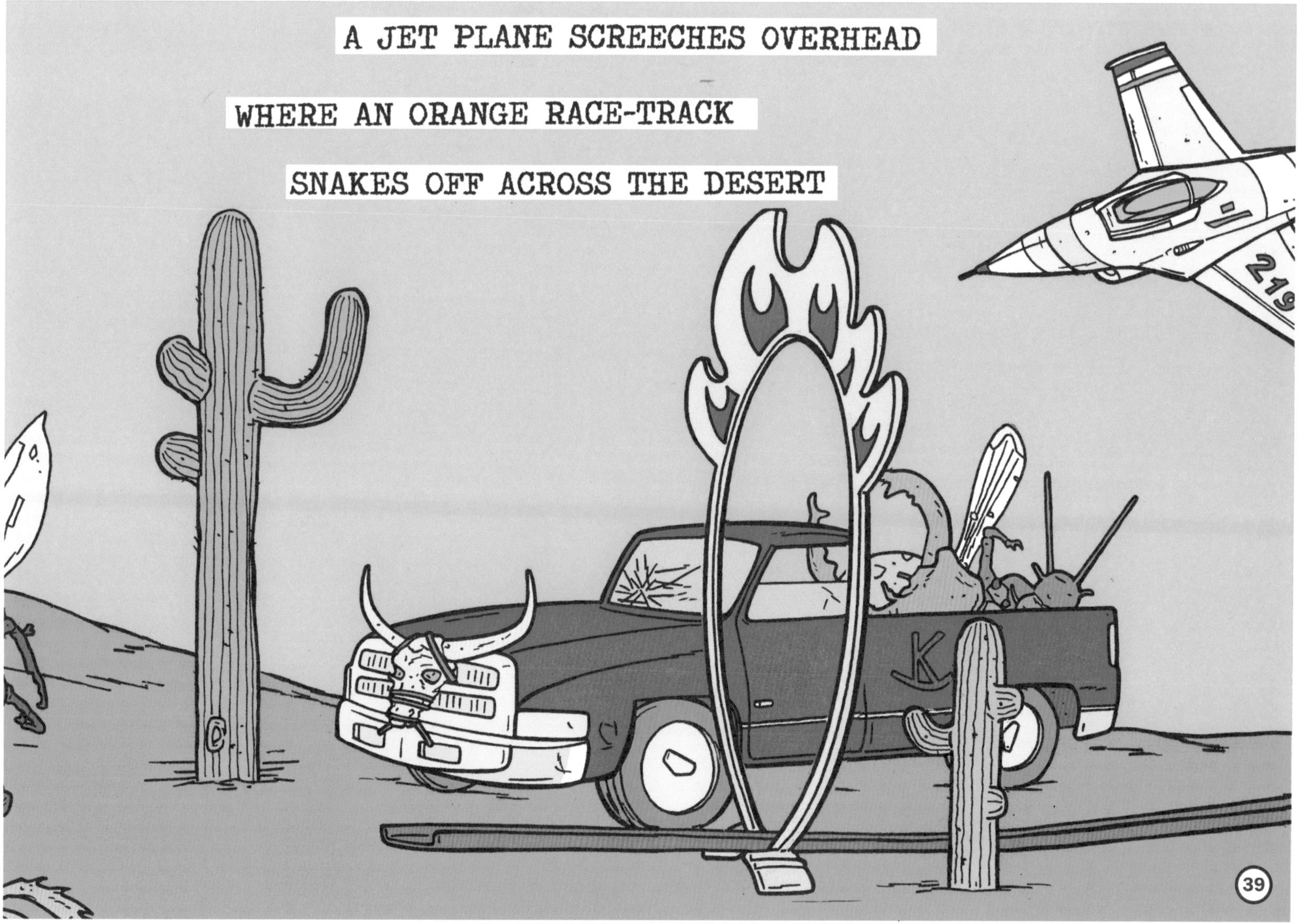
A JET PLANE SCREECHES OVERHEAD
WHERE AN ORANGE RACE-TRACK
SNAKES OFF ACROSS THE DESERT
219
K

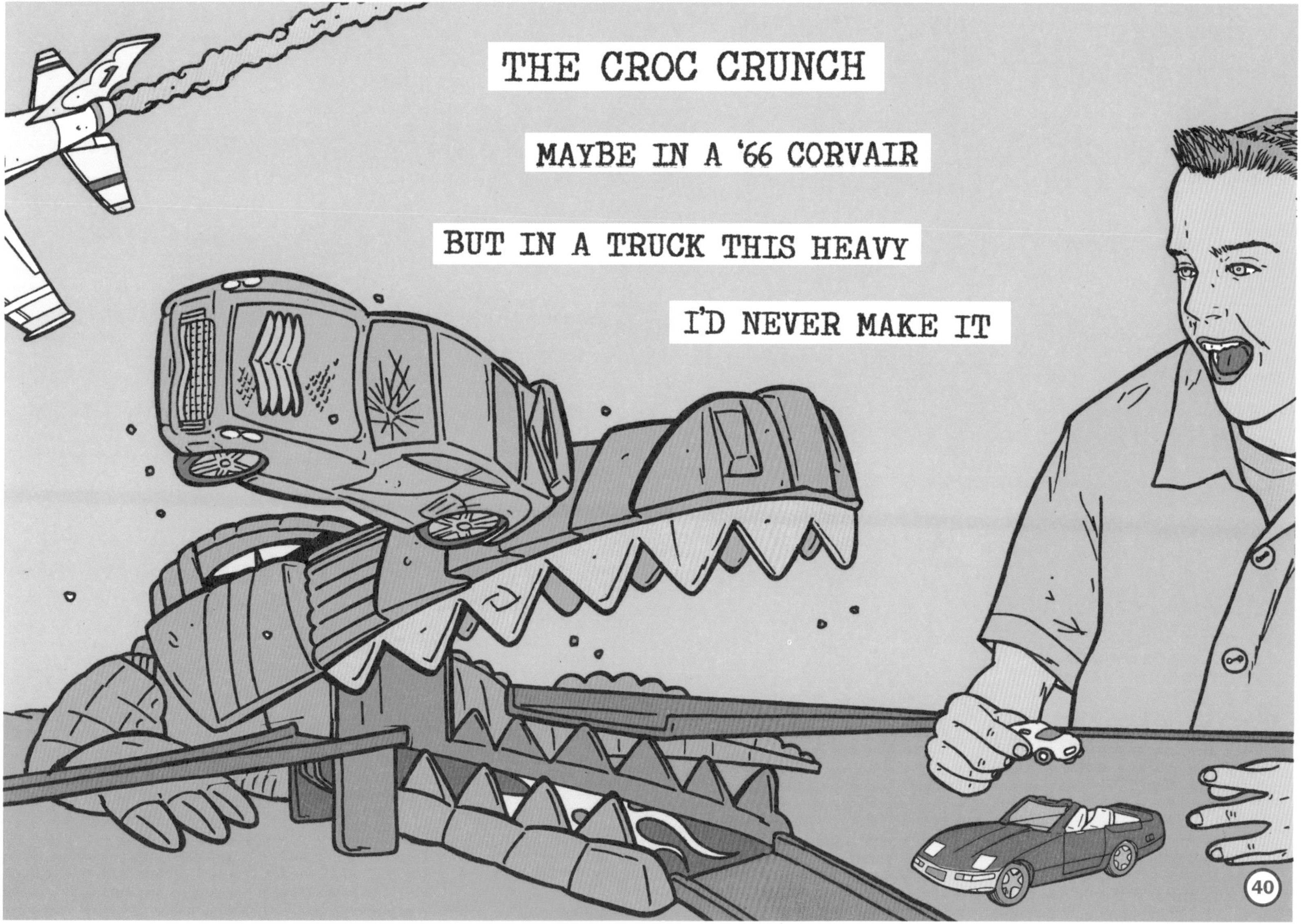
THE CROC CRUNCH
MAYBE IN A '66 CORVAIR
BUT IN A TRUCK THIS HEAVY
I'D NEVER MAKE IT

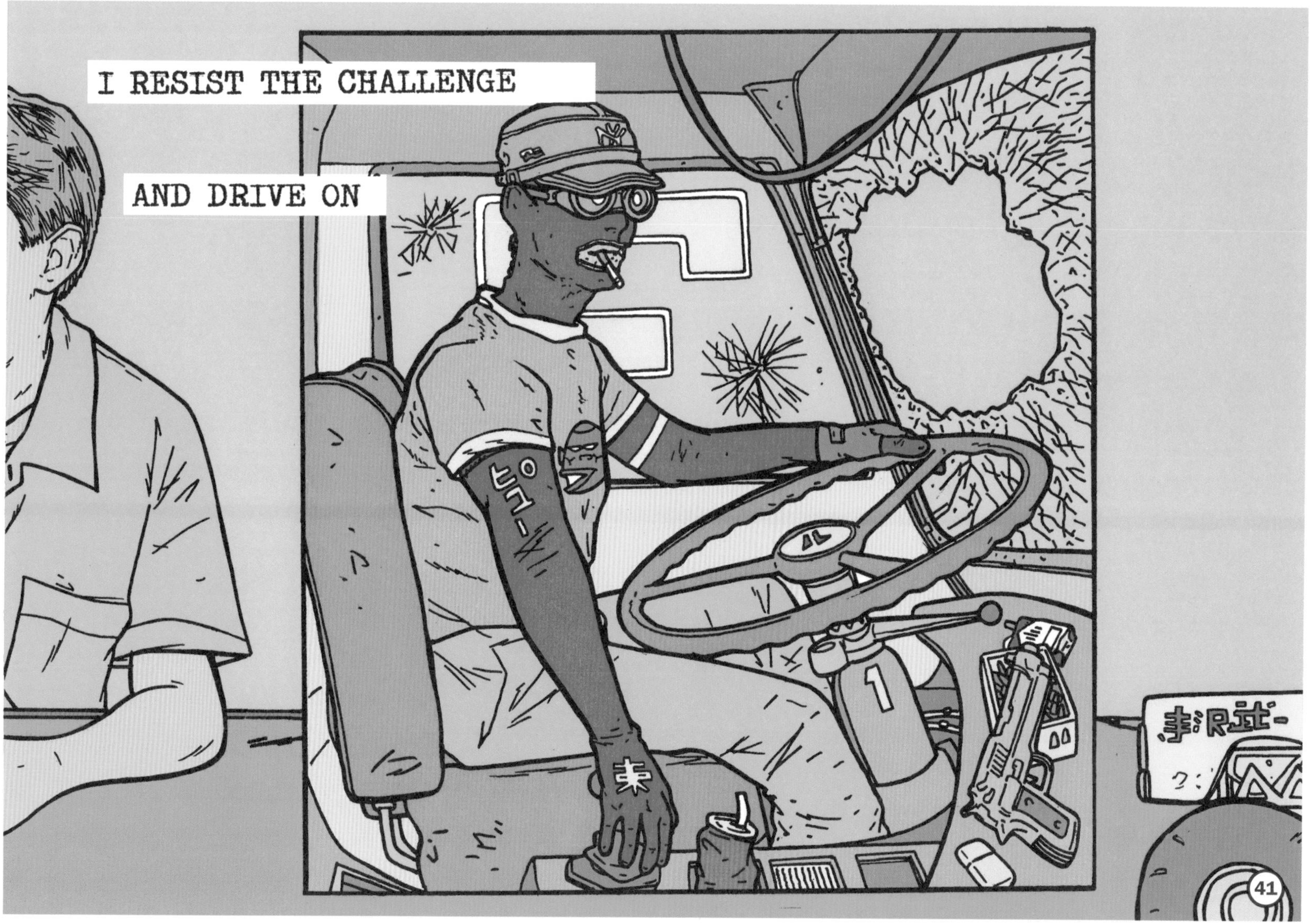
I RESIST THE CHALLENGE
AND DRIVE ON

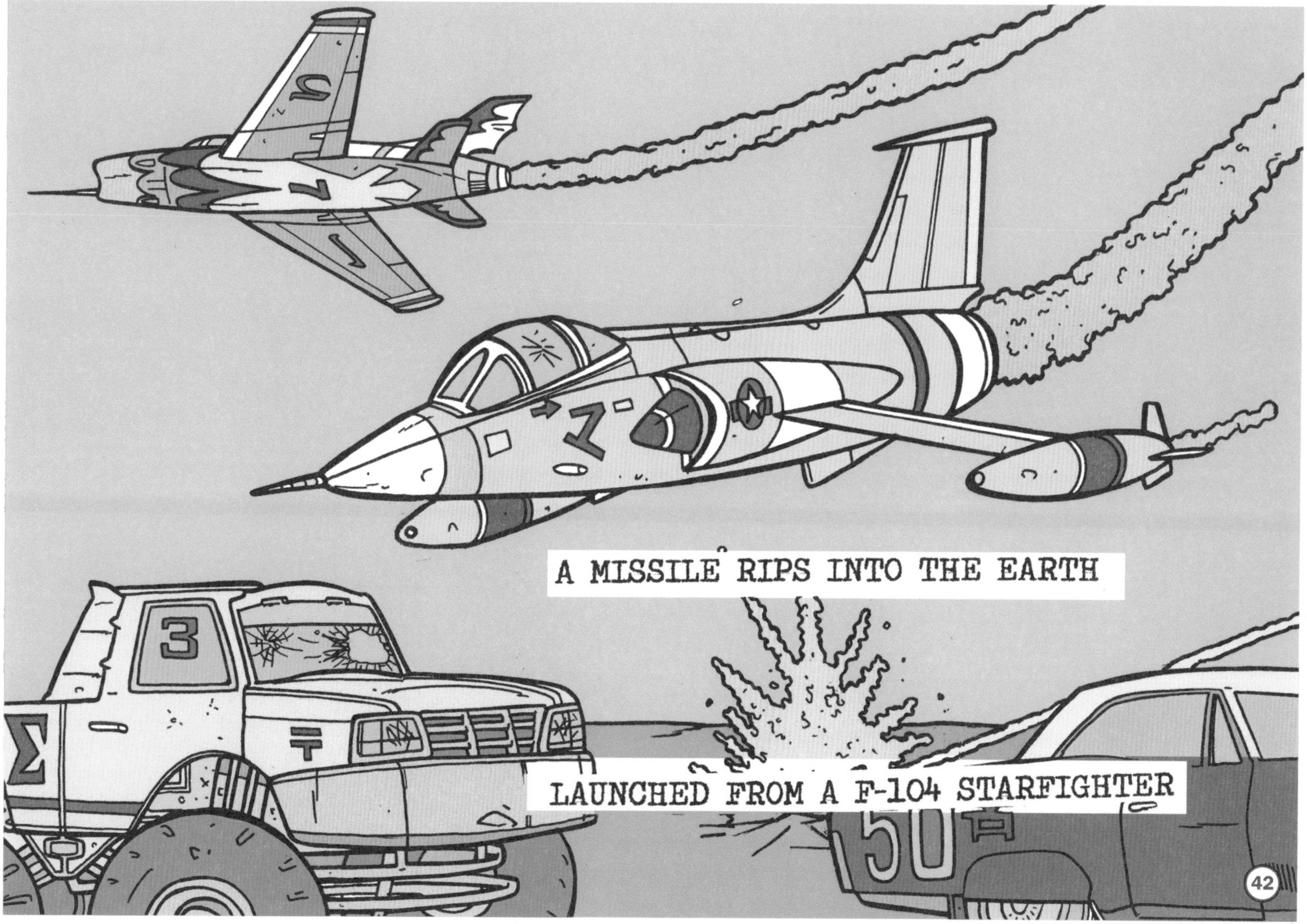
A MISSILE RIPS INTO THE EARTH
LAUNCHED FROM A F-104 STARFIGHTER

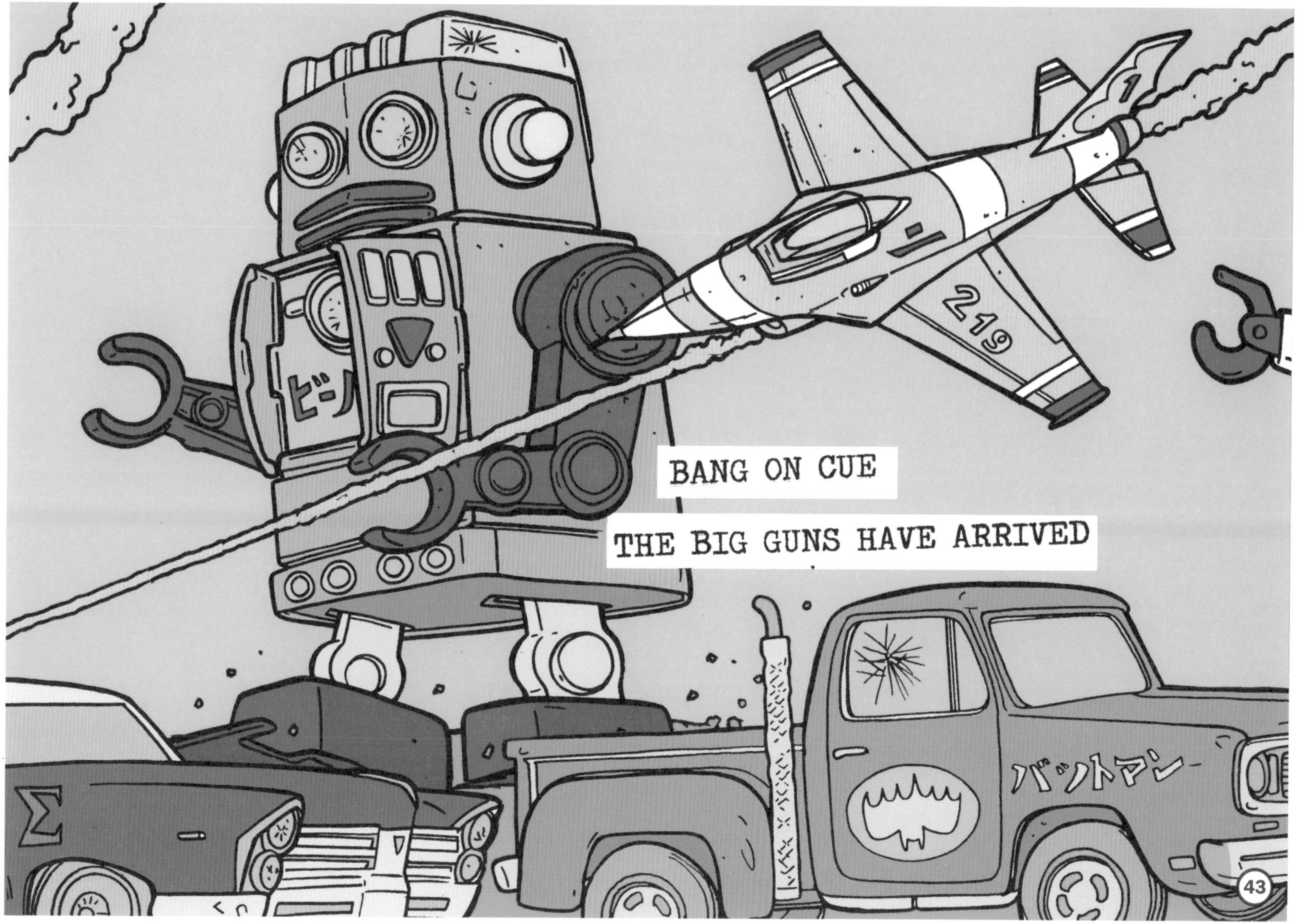
BANG ON CUE
THE BIG GUNS HAVE ARRIVED
219
バットマン

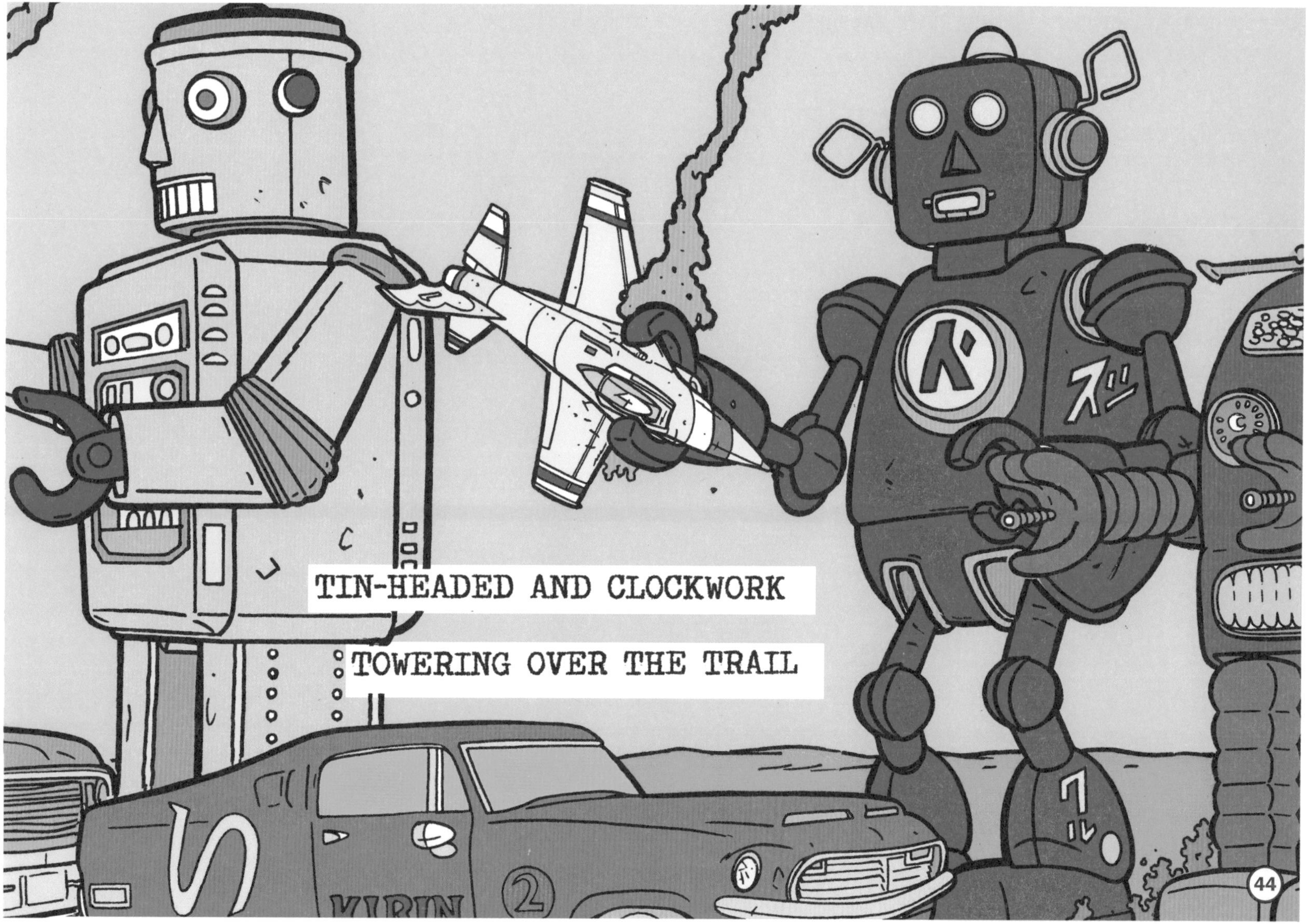
TIN-HEADED AND CLOCKWORK
TOWERING OVER THE TRAIL

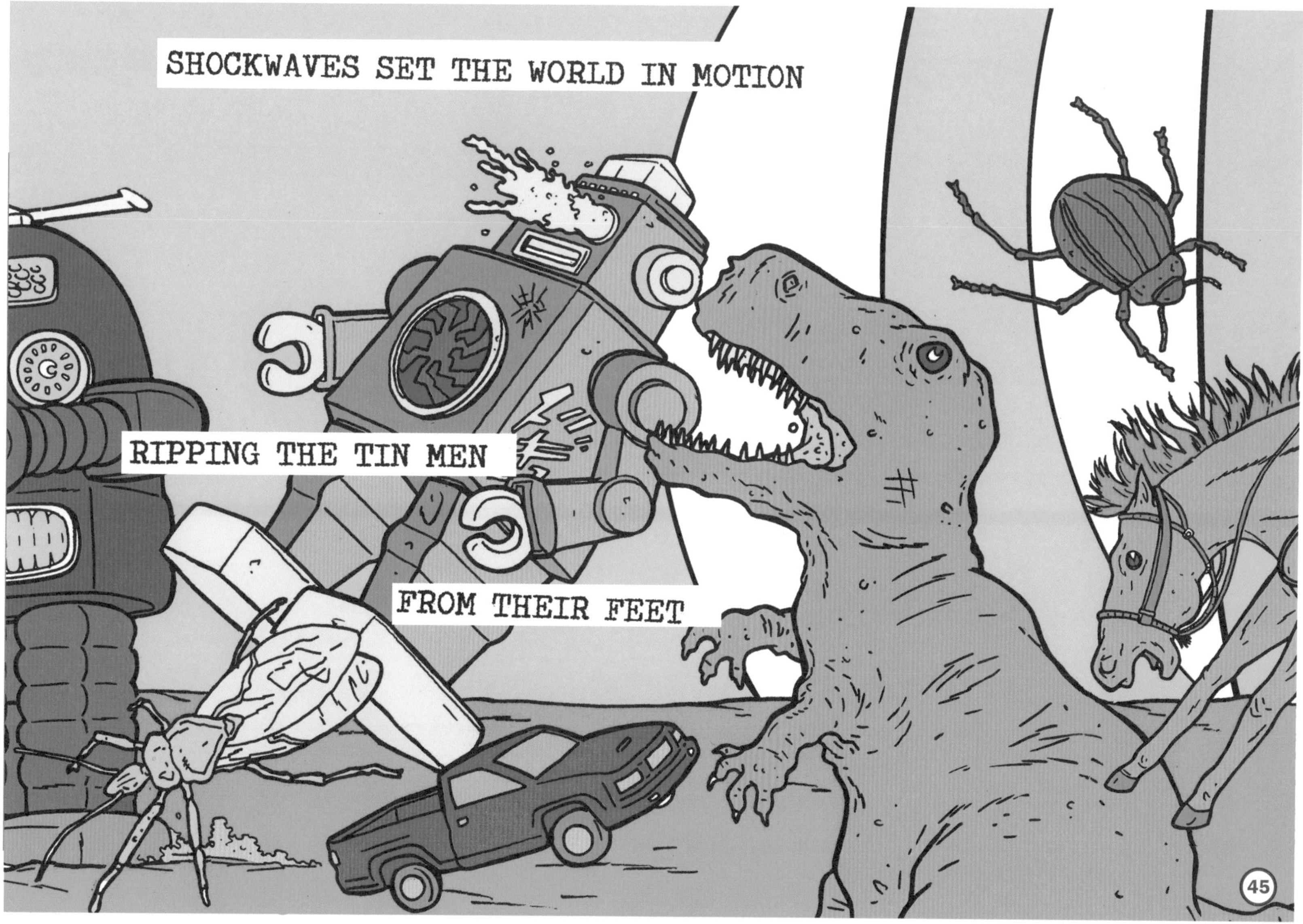
SHOCKWAVES SET THE WORLD IN MOTION
RIPPING THE TIN MEN
FROM THEIR FEET

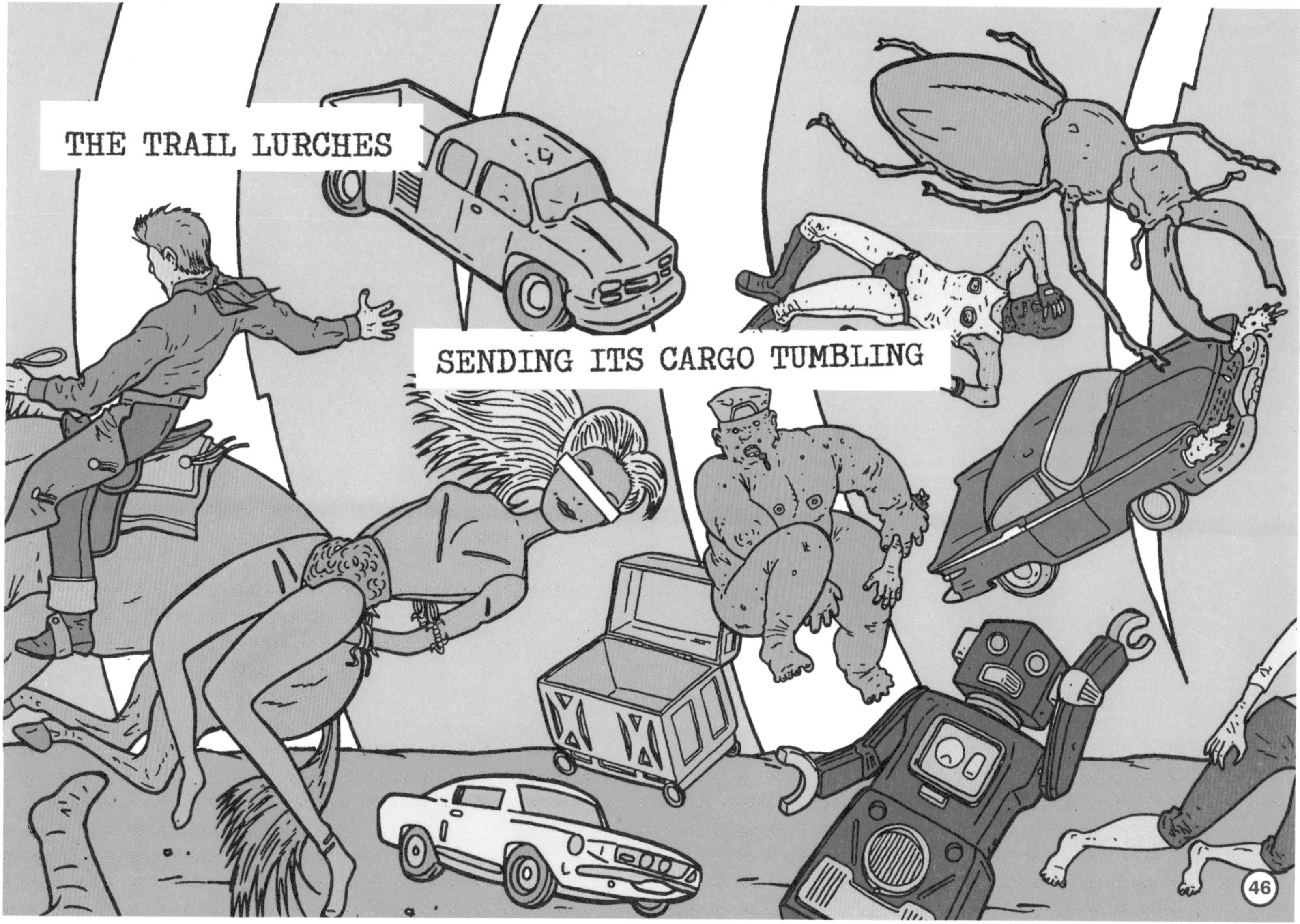
THE TRAIL LURCHES
SENDING ITS CARGO TUMBLING

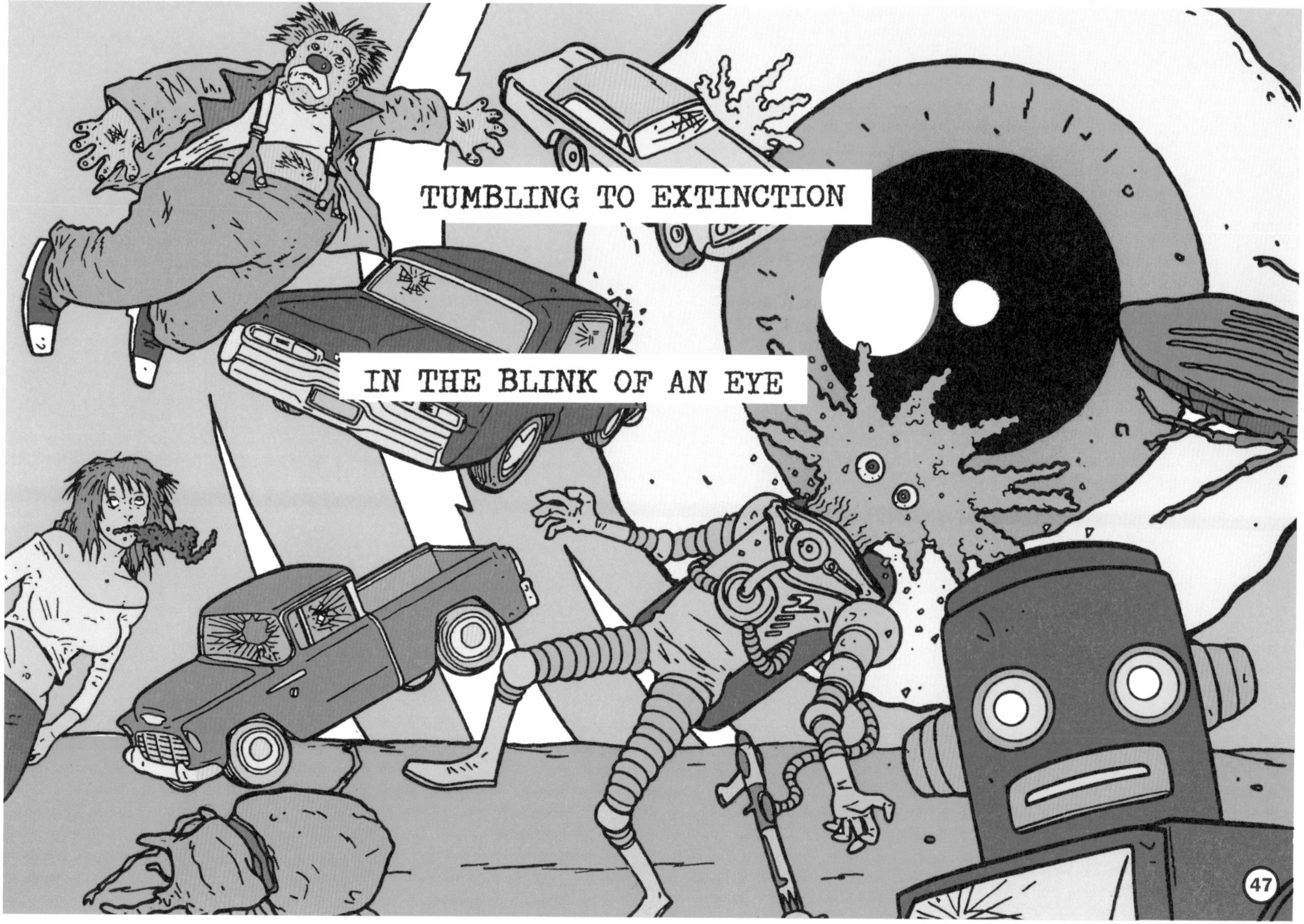
TUMBLING TO EXTINCTION
IN THE BLINK OF AN EYE

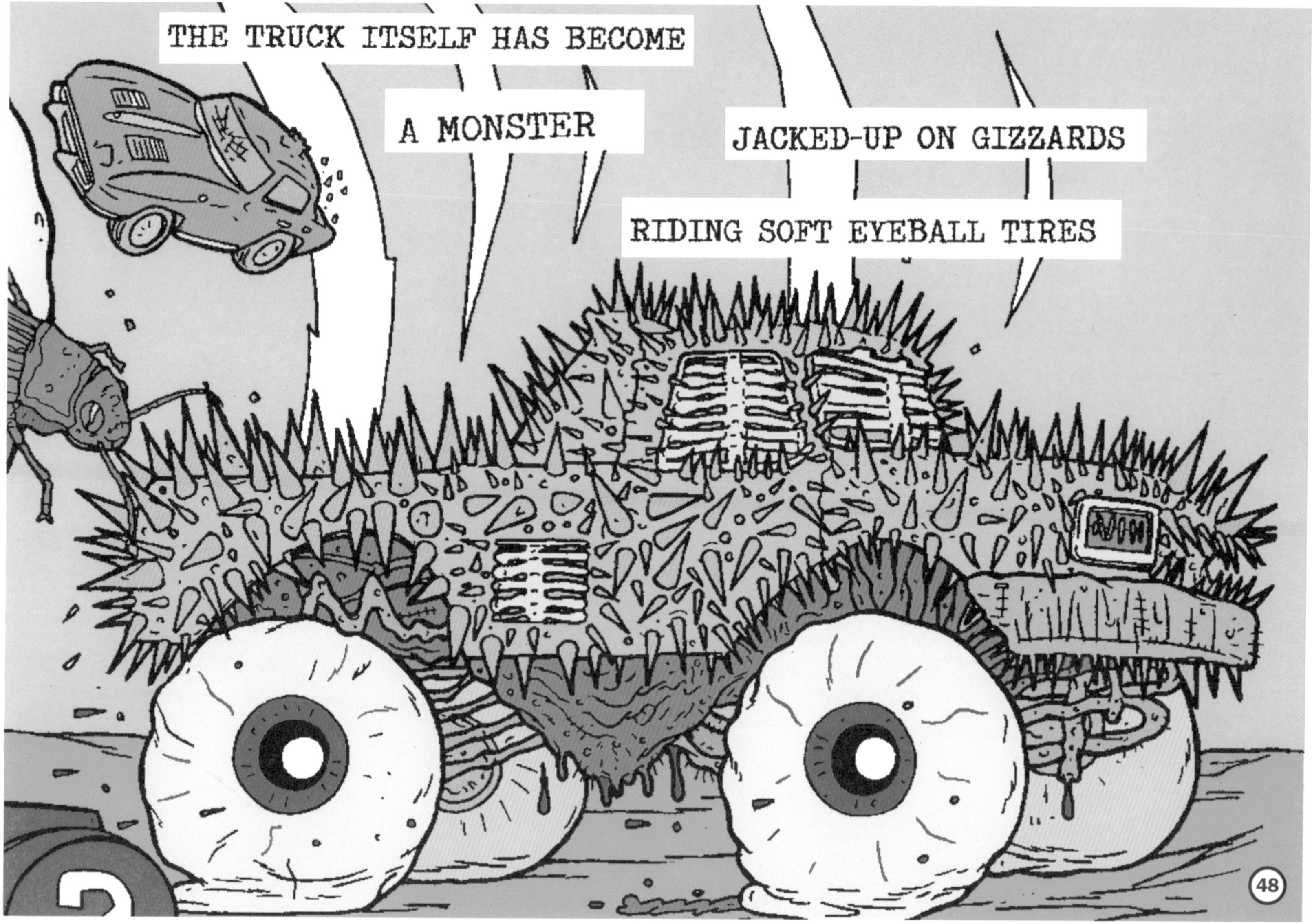
THE TRUCK ITSELF HAS BECOME
A MONSTER
JACKED-UP ON GIZZARDS
RIDING SOFT EYEBALL TIRES

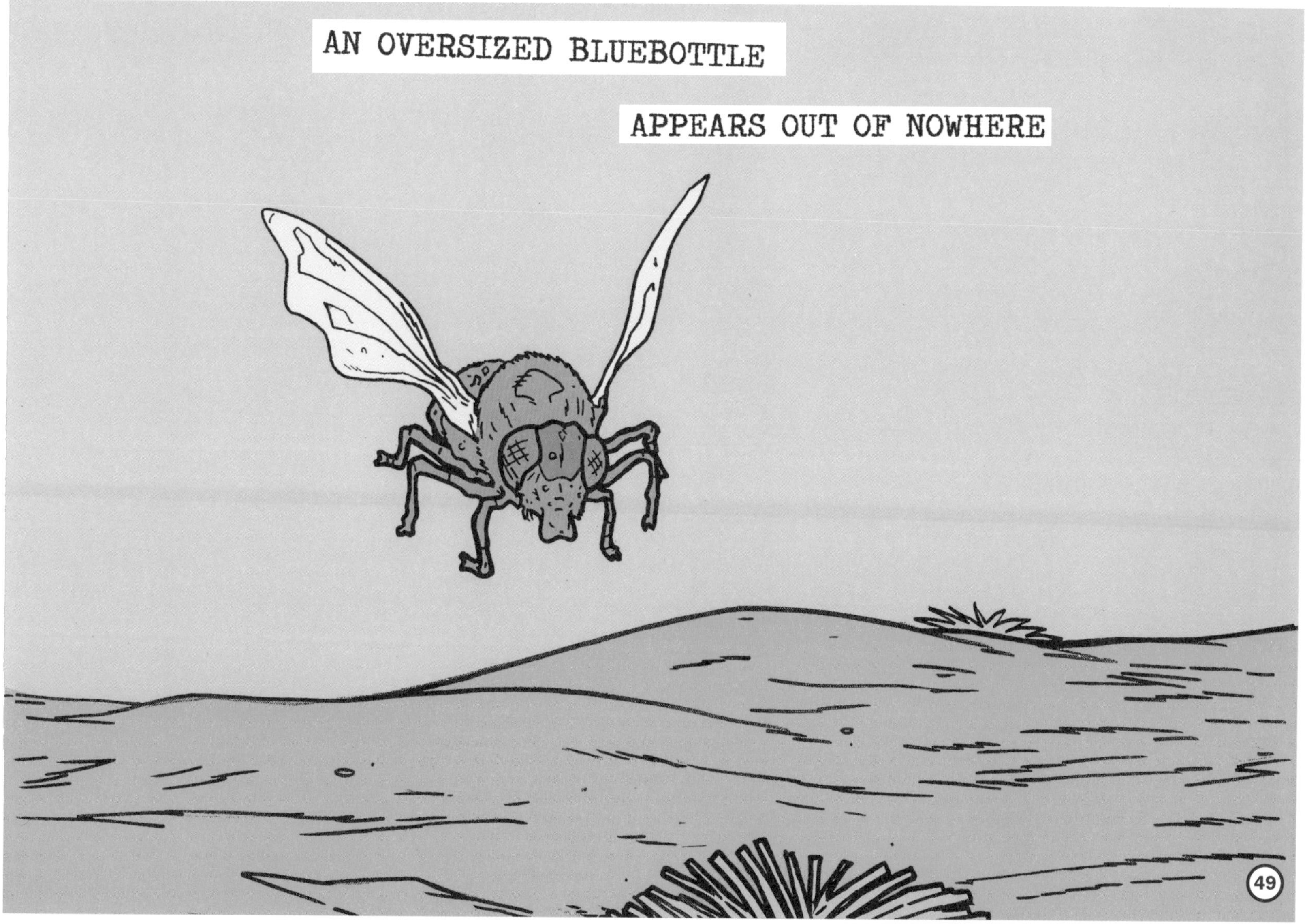
AN OVERSIZED BLUEBOTTLE
APPEARS OUT OF NOWHERE

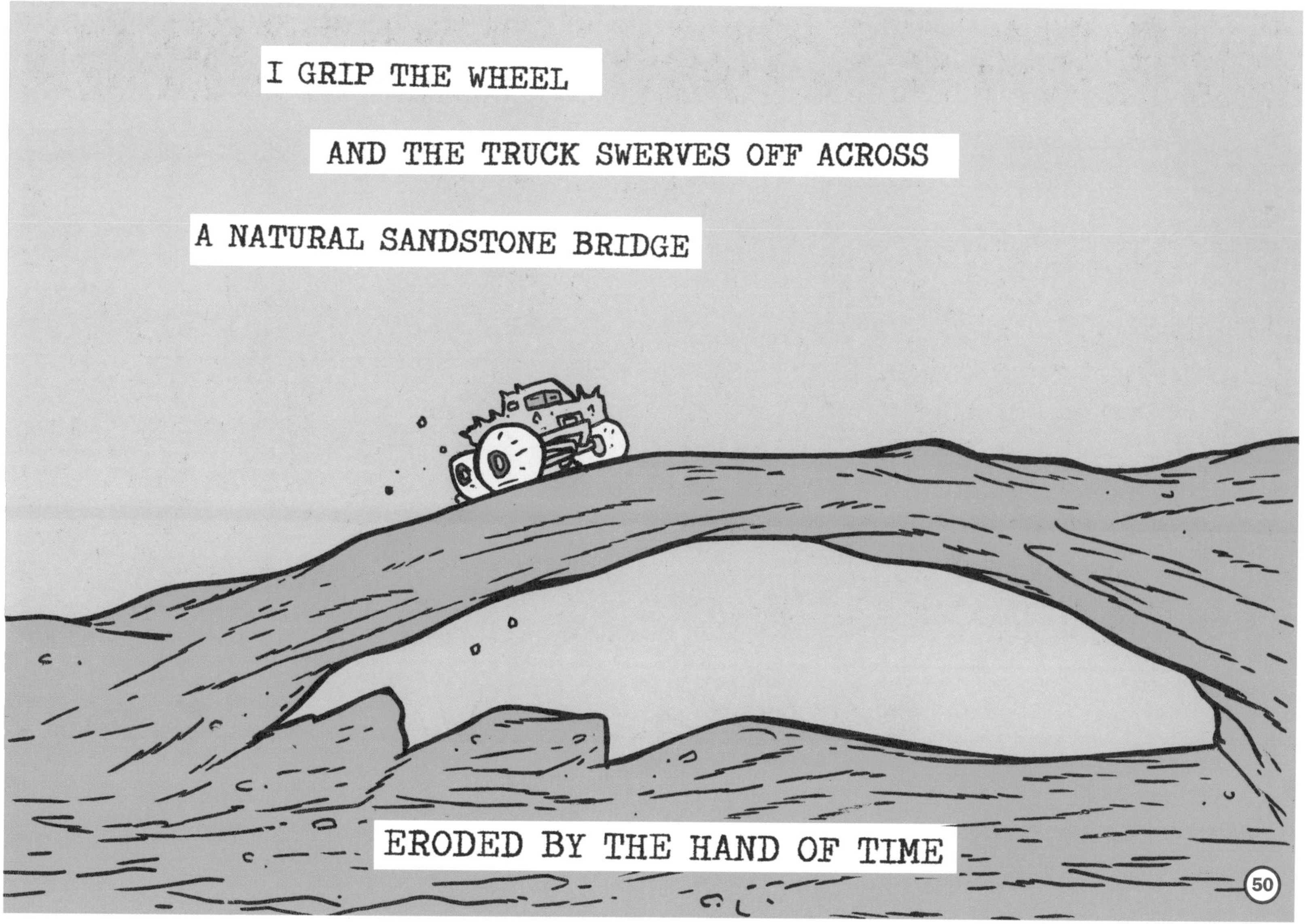
I GRIP THE WHEEL
AND THE TRUCK SWERVES OFF ACROSS
A NATURAL SANDSTONE BRIDGE
ERODED BY THE HAND OF TIME

REAR VIEW MIRROR

AMT Ertl, Edward Hopper, Chevy, Ford Motors, Ford Bigfoot, Corvette, Diamond Rio, NASA, Ford Louisville, Hasbro, Mattel, Dorling Kindersley, La Rocka! Di Londres, Plymouth 'Cuda, DC Comics, Topps Company, George Adamski, Jump Japan, Frederick J. Garner, Usborne How To Draw Buildings, Universal Studios, George Barris, Dean R. Koontz, Richard Laymon, Bobo, Taschen, Ladybird, Jack 'King' Kirby, McDonald Educational, Lockheed, Coca Cola, Ozzie's Robots, Geof Darrow, Richard Starkings, JG Roshell, Eric Stephenson.

With special thanks to Paul Vincent for his support on this project.

FOR LAURIE AND KITTY, TRAVEL COMPANIONS